NATURAL LAW

NATURAL LAW

UNIVERSAL IN SCOPE
MORAL IN DESIGN

◇◇◇◇◇◇◇◇◇◇◇◇◇◇◇◇◇◇◇◇◇◇◇◇◇◇◇◇

THE BIBLICAL DOCTRINE OF
AVAILABLE LIGHT

◇◇◇◇◇◇◇◇◇◇◇◇◇◇◇◇◇◇◇◇◇◇◇◇◇◇◇◇◇◇◇◇

BY STANLEY W. PAHER

NEVADA PUBLICATIONS
4135 Badger Circle • Reno, Nevada 89519

NATURAL LAW
Universal in Scope
Moral in Design

ISBN: 0-913814-93-8

Published by **NEVADA PUBLICATIONS**
4135 Badger Circle, Reno, Nevada 89519
spaher@sbcglobal.net

First Printing , 1998
Reprinted 2004
Revised and enlarged, May, 2010

PROUDLY PRINTED IN THE UNITED STATES OF AMERICA

More than an author of popular western history, Stanley W. Paher has written six other books on various religious topics, including the subject of covenant, kingdom, a commentary on Matthew Chapter 24, the Babylon concept in the Book of Revelation, religious psychology, and the subject of the the nature and person of God. He currently lives in Reno where he is working on other western and religious subjects.

TABLE OF CONTENTS

◇◇◇◇◇◇◇◇◇◇◇◇◇◇◇◇◇◇◇◇◇

~ CHAPTER ONE ~

INTRODUCTION TO NATURAL LAW

Immutable Natural Law consists of one supreme universal principle, the unfolding of God's orderly universe, and is founded on the creation and the very nature of man. From it is derived all moral obligations and duties, rules of conduct which have been prescribed to us by the Creator in the conscience of everyone who has ever lived. Natural Law culminates in Jesus Christ who is central to this revelation of God, for his blood flows to cover the sins of all righteous people, anytime and anywhere, before and after the cross. People from all of the nations are amenable to the same recognizable moral standard, and it is firmly rooted in the character of God.

Everyone who has ever lived is subject to Natural Law and it will serve as the basis of end-time judgment for all, whether living before or after the cross, or in or out of a formal covenant with God and saved by the gospel of Christ. Moral-thinking people are characterized by an impulse for rightness and justice, equity, fundamental fairness, virtue. Revelation 5:9 shows that people from the entire compass of time will be redeemed by Christ's blood. His life was a sacrificial offer for the sins of all mankind. Blessed by this universal atoning is a countless throng standing erect, confident, triumphant. Another large group who reject morality and the existence and the Creator live in utter darkness, and await the horror of judgment.

A third way in which God has disclosed His will is special revelation to His covenant people through the apostles, prophets and other holy men of old. God's mind and will was ultimately set forth in canonical documents, the present Bible, first to the Old Testament Jews and now to those submitting to the gospel of Christ.

Special revelation thus joins Natural Law where the Creator-God has forever revealed Himself to mankind in two harmoniously interacting ways: generally in the creative order, and in the consciences of all men, realms subject to ever-present physical and moral laws, all of which are based on the integrity of God.

These twin sources—general and special revelation—complement each other like hand in glove, disclosing the nature and purpose of God and His redemptive plan for mankind. Both of these heaven-originated types of revelation center upon universal truths, and each can, if respected, bring acceptability and blessings. General revelation is the older, universal disclosure of God's mind and will to every human being who has ever lived, while special revelation, God's supernatural disclosure of truth to prophets and apostles, is directed to a small segment of mankind—to covenant people uniquely furnished with the Old and New Testaments.

The promise to the ancient patriarch Abraham of a universal blessing to all nations (Gen.12-15-17) has the special revelation of the Bible as its corner-stone. Apart from it is the Natural Law of general revelation which furnishes vital truths to all including non-covenanters—people who stand before God either approved or rejected, based on their inward attitude toward their available light: acknowledgement of the Creator and the inner sense of ought within the law in the heart, as developed in Chapter Five.

God's special apostolic and prophetic revelation is like carefully controlled laser light, beaming exclusively upon a mere fraction of humanity: at first covenant Jews and now Christians, baptized believers after the cross. It discloses to all of them the Abrahamic blessing of remission of sin and a salvation which was ultimately perfected through Jesus Christ.

In contrast, every person whether in or out of a formal covenant with God confronts at every turn in life God's Natural Law to mankind: the universal revelation of Himself in the creation's orderliness and the moral realm where there are right and wrong ways embedded in the conscience of everyone. This revelation is like ambient or broadly naturally occurring physical light which continually shines upon every one, past, present and future. The non-covenanters' standing before God is based solely upon positive response to this general revelation, and it serves as their present truth and basis for end-time judgment, as explained in Chapter Seven.

Jesus Christ rules as Lord over both general and special revelation. He is the light who furnishes truth to every man generally, but his special mission was to shine upon called-out people through his apostles, precisely as God had revealed His mind and will to covenant Jews of old by His servants, the prophets. General and special revelation harmonize in marvelous unity, since each is an expression of the word of God and of the creation's moral order.

Studying the doctrine of Natural Law is not merely an academic pursuit. It has as its foundation proper character and respect for God, ethical considerations bound up in morality, and heart-obedience to known truths. Since God has spoken about this subject and has furnished guidance, we must adhere. Natural Law touches upon God's grace, mercy and favor, and His righteous judgment as the created search for Him in their available light, truth at hand. This doctrine is no small matter and is certainly worth investigation. Christians should be willing to study it and make positive application of Natural Law with respect to spreading the gospel of Christ, not only to the generally illiterate parts of the world, but also in Western nations which have access to gospel preaching and benefit from Bible study. In these twin ways, God's for redemptive purposes are fully shown and would not be misrepresented.

THE ESSENCE OF NATURAL LAW

Natural Law, also known as the "law in the heart," universal law, moral law, and Adamic law, directly relates to morals and ethics—actions and behavior of men toward each other, which may be virtuous or unjust, good or bad. This universally applicable law, spanning every age and culture, embraces what is morally right in the very nature of man's relationship with others and with God, overflowing from the holiness of the Creator Himself. It is an expression of the unchanging mind and will of God and His plan for man. Violation of this high moral standard is sin, a definite transgression or wrong against God's universal order of things.

Natural Law is part of the "truth of God" (Rom. 1:25, John 3:21). It is consistent with the creation and character of God and is fully in accord with prophetic and apostolic teaching preserved in Scripture. God will judge impartially and benevolently all who embrace the light accorded them; those who repel truths known and understood will be rejected in Heaven's court. Light (truth) brings responsibility (Jas. 3:1).

Ethical principles, laws, and truths in a moral realm exist because God created a conscience as an inherent part of every man. It is an awareness which uniquely discriminates between a "right way" and a "wrong way." Unless the conscience is seared, it has a tendency to do the right (see Chapter Four). As aptly stated by H. C. Theissen, conscience "is a reflection of God in the soul. Just as the lake's [smooth surface] reflects the sun and reveals not only its existence, but also to some extent its nature, so conscience in man reveals both the existence of God and to some extent the nature of God" (*Systematic Theology*, p. 35).

Denial of the existence of conscience and a moral realm governed by God amounts to renouncing reality and turning one's back on the obvious.

Throughout history, moral and ethical principles have essentially been the same, for such eternal truths are solidly based upon eternal justice and the very character and being of the unchangeable Creator. Certain actions are offensive against God's nature. Since lying, idolatry, murder, adultery, rebellion, murmuring, and the like are wrong for every man, God's moral system is not subject to reinterpretation among various earthly societies throughout history.

When the apostles and prophets set forth moral teaching in Scripture, they did not arbitrarily declare that specific deeds and thoughts were wrong, hence sinful. Rather, these practices of man against man were *already* wrong, bad ever since the time of Genesis three. They violate the equal rights of man, which is the basis of all human justice. Natural Law is of God, because fairness and righteousness envelops His nature.

No person (or even a political entity) determines what is right and wrong. He merely recognizes these things. In the course of daily living, everyone must decide how to react to each of life's situations. The critical items of character, maintaining relationships, and honoring commitments are within the sphere of the freedom to choose. Since negative willful acts result in mental or physical pain to others, a general knowledge of the wrongness of the deliberate hurting of another is basic to human nature.

People in all past or present cultures can arrive at God's moral standard by asking. "How do I want others to behave towards me," or "How do others want to be treated?" The Golden Rule becomes evident, as well as the duty to love. This includes the proper recognition of and respect for God (Matt. 22:37-38; Mic. 6:8; Hos. 6:6). Simply restated, the bases for duty which the Creator requires of His creation are love of God first, then love of neighbor.

Any rational, conscientious person capable of understanding right from the wrong can recognize moral duty and proper behavior. Stealing, murder, covetousness, greed, malice, etc. are not rendered wrong because of the Bible, but are inherently wrong in every place and are contrary to God's mind and will, His unwritten divine moral plan for man. Evil people of any age who practice immorality live in darkness and flee from the light (John 3:19), ignoring the actual, the virtuous, the good part, thus denying the moral truth and whatever light is "in... them" (Rom. 1:20). Conversely, all who do the truth come to the light of goodness and reality. At any moment in time, with no respect to culture or religion, all people are either approaching light or darkness, enhancing or suppressing whatever truth is within them.

Universal Natural Law is based on thoughts and deeds which are the proper things to do for every man. It is natural for a mother to bear children, to care for them (and not to injure a child or abort a fetus). It is natural to seek marriage; it is contrary to nature to divorce a mate, to "forbid marriage" (I Tim. 4:1-3), attempt suicide, or engage in homosexuality. It is natural to protect one's life and family; it is unnatural to allow evildoers to take life or not defend a home when one can ward off an intruder by misstating the truth of the whereabouts of innocent family members, or stealing his weapon or even killing him. Natural Law is both enlightening and condemning, and is undergirded by evenhandedness.

THE DIVINE SOURCE OF NATURAL LAW

Universal moral law is how God reveals Himself to enlighten every man. It is rooted in God's efficiently designed creation and His moral order. It is His universal self-enforcing law of absolute right, calling for straight thinking and appropriate behavior on the part of everyone throughout time. Natural Law calls for positive, rational thought and moral choices—no matter the situation or circumstance. Right actions get right results; wrong actions bring wrong results.

Moral behavior is foundational to God's overall desires, purposes, and plan for man. Natural Law's divine source is displayed in universal right and wrong, in doing good and refraining from evil. An honest response to this truth always assumes responsibility for its dealings with fellow man, and never blames wrong results on other people, inherited genes, bad luck, or any other excuse.

The origin of moral norms is imparted by the creation, and expresses itself in the rational structure of human judgment and actions. Natural Law genuinely addresses both the positive and negative actions of all. Neither the Christian nor non-Christian can always do the good that should be done, but either can at all times refuse to do evil.

Man is not his own legislator. He is to follow his God-given available light and never walk in darkness. God's law of nature teaches that there are a number of intrinsically evil deeds, among them homicide, genocide, abortion, trafficking in women and children. When is rape morally justified? Atrocities like Auschwitz? Or the torture of children, the aged or others made in the image of God? Circumstances may mitigate personal responsibility, but these acts forever remain bad, always and in every place. The works of the flesh are plain, as catalogued in Galatians 5:19-21.

A right-thinking person is prepared to sacrifice anything rather than to carry out an evil. Apt are the words of the Roman poet Juvenal: "Consider it the greatest of crimes to prefer survival to honor and, out of love of physical life, to lose the very reason for living." Though most people are not called to martyrdom, they are obligated to bear witness to their measure of known truth. That is what it means to live in available light. Here is freedom.

Every function of nature is the result of God's agency. The laws of nature are responsible for everything—the orderliness and the design of the four seasons, the rain which falls upon lands which burst forth with new life, the flow of rivers and the roll of oceans, the revolution of the sun and the stars in the heavens. All of these and more testify of Natural Law. Our Creator—He is alive! And as shown in the 8th Psalm, God has concern for all human beings by lavishly providing for them moral orderliness which, when followed by anyone, brings goodness and life, acceptance. Salvation is not accorded to those who persist in evil and reject their understood truth of God, which is righteousness, justice, kindness, love, etc. These are revealed in the natural order of things, as disclosed in Romans 1:18-19.

In contrast, those who have yet to come to a greater understanding about God's will—His plan and purposes for man through Jesus Christ—are nevertheless "doing truth," for "he that practices the truth cometh to the light" (John 3:21, Rom. 1:25). Such are "of God" because people living by His light as generally revealed to them are accounted as righteous and justified by faith, just as are Christians. Faith is faith. These good hearts actively serve the living God in their truth as presently understood. As no respecter of persons, God ever takes note of moral character.

There are currently millions of people—indeed, there have always been—who have lesser light than that which has been made available to Christians. Though people unexposed to the gospel do not personally know Jesus, the Light of the world, and may never see a Bible nor hear an evangelist, assuredly they are not bereft of natural moral guidance and access to God. To one and all, God has not left Himself without witness (Acts 14:17). Their light is the universal moral order and the design of nature, and these are their teachers (Psalm 19:1-6; cp. Rom. 10:18).

Everyone who casts aside this light by choosing to live for self through indifference to right and wrong, willful ignorance, or maintain a rebellious spirit, will be rejected by the One who has provided them positive measures of guidance. Regardless of the brightness or dimness of the light, all people have a choice; they will either seek and accept the good, or ignore and reject, and God will dispense either immortality or spiritual death.

GOD'S CONCERN FOR GOOD-HEARTED NON-COVENANT PEOPLE.

Throughout the last 2000 years, among every nation and people group, there are untold numbers of God-seekers who, through no fault of their own, have never had an opportunity to hear and respond to the gospel of Jesus Christ. These moral God-fearers have lived and died never specifically knowing of the person and mission of the Son of God. They do not willfully reject him—they simply have no oral or written knowledge of him. What is the status of these good hearts before God? Can they enjoy a present acceptance (salvation) based on Natural Law, respecting God and conscientiously doing what is morally right?

Both the Old and New Testaments furnish a considerable amount of positive information about scores of right-thinking people who seek God and live rightly, based on limited knowledge of His will. They follow the light that is accorded them, the reality of the creation and moral order in Natural Law, and do not reject additional truth if it were presented to them. Though many Christians conclude that the principle of available light as applied to salvation is decidedly speculative, they are apparently unaware that God has not left us uninformed about the present status and eternal destiny of these believers who live according to God's moral standard.

Responsibility comes once God has drawn individuals to that measure of light as stated in Luke 12:48b: "To whom much as been given, more is required of them." No sin accrues in not having heard the word of Christ. To his disciples he said, "If I had not come and spoken to them, they would not have sin, but now [that they have heard] they have no excuse for their sin" (John 15:22, see also v. 24). Judgment enters at the point of rejecting Christ's teaching and not before, because those blameless ones spoken of by Jesus in these verses had not yet had the opportunity to hear and accept the greater light of the gospel. They are disposed to hear the voice of the Saviour (John 8:47; see also Chapter Twelve).

All people, past present and future, are responsible to that measure of light (available truth) which God has given to them. As the Father of all light (Jas. 1:17; cp. I Pet. 2:9-10, I John 1:5), imagery borrowed from the heavenly stars, God respects those who are following the light presently accorded them while seeking and not rejecting additional truth. God's light ranges from a rudimentary belief in the Creator and the reality of moral standards to the advanced and fuller truths embodied in special biblical revelation. And so, every person through God's grace and protection receives some measure of eternal truths about God. This law written on the heart is his present available light. Our just, loving, merciful God does not judge a person for not knowing truth which he had no way of discovering and with no opportunity to properly respond.

The coming of Jesus did not change man's inner nature; it was the same before and after the cross to everyone whether under Moses or Christ. Covenanted ones have no monopoly on humility, good will, openness, honesty, courage, and other positive traits stemming from pure hearts and clear consciences. Indeed, by virtue of God's abundant grace, all persons have some light (truth) available to them, and every person is responsible for the degree of the knowledge they possess about God. There are no exceptions.

Righteous individuals have been around since ancient times, and even today the faithful under Natural Law enjoy the status of being "excused," secure before God (Rom. 2:14-15). The virtuous with an acceptable faith have access to the blood of Christ, the exclusive agent to cover sin. Therefore, all God-fearers outside of a formal covenant need not feel that there is an unbridgeable gulf between themselves and God, for they are righteous people as well, approaching God in the best way they know how, living faithfully to their available light.

CHAPTER TWO

ROMANS ONE:
THE SHOWCASE
OF NATURAL LAW

The most extensive biblical expression of Natural Law in the Bible is taught by Paul in Romans 1-2. Specifically 1:18-20 plainly teaches that what can be known about God is manifest in all men, because God has disclosed it to them. Ever since the world began, His invisible nature and eternal power and divinity, have been clearly perceived in the created universe. So the unrighteous are without excuse for not knowing about God.

Clearly, the apostle declared that all men possess knowledge of God's nature and the moral realm. God gave it to all men; it did not come from preaching Christ or written Scripture, special revelation. This awareness of the creation and a broad sense of morality are engraved upon the mind—"in" them and "to" them. (v. 19). It is plainly perceived; it is universally applicable in every situation by virtue of common humanity. This non-codified, unwritten law in the heart and mind furnishes everyone a general, unspecified standard for acceptable behavior. Romans 1:20, 25 expressly state that there is no excuse for being unaware of God and not respecting moral acts and precepts.

In Romans 1:18-32, the apostle Paul thoroughly describes the reality of universal Natural Law, contrasting righteous people who recognize God's work in creation and His moral law with evildoers who smother the truth in unrighteousness by engaging in pernicious, ungodly actions. The evidence of God's wholehearted acceptance of faithful Gentiles, non-covenant people, is developed more fully in Romans 2, in the concept of the law in the heart (see Chapter Five).

THE WRATH OF GOD

R omans 1:18 states: "For the wrath of God is revealed from heaven against all ungodliness and unrighteousness of men, who suppress the truth in unrighteousness." The word "for" invites a contrast with verse 17, which announces the good news of a personal, omnipotent Creator-God extending His righteousness to all just people who live by the principle of faith. The bad news of verse 18 is that God's wrath will be brought forth against all ungodliness and the unrighteousness of everyone who pushes away or holds down the truth through harmful deeds and evil ways.

The hindering or hiding of God's light is depicted in the figure of a wicked man putting truth in a box and sitting on the lid (Robertson, *Word Pictures, in the New Testament*, 4:328). The wrath signifies an indignation not boiling up in violent divine temper, but something which has risen gradually as a flower bud cracks slowly before its blooming (Robertson, 4:327; Hendrickson, *Commentary on Romans*, p. 372). It is not mere angry divine vengeance, but the eternal repulsion of evil by good.

"Wrath revealed from heaven" is not brought about by the revealed gospel written down by the apostles, but is heaven-sent wrath through the simplicity of cause and effect of nature's laws and activity (Shepard, *Life and Letters of Paul*, p. 372). It is directed against all irrationality, injustice and unfairness. As a result, God gives over men (*paradidonai*) to cook in their own juices as a divine intervention (see W. E. Vine, *Expository Dictionary of New Testament Words*, p. 489). This wrath does not extend to anyone who recognizes the Creator and learns to love, honor and trust Him and adhere to His moral principles, as embodied in Natural Law.

The concept of ungodliness, as displayed in an anti-God attitude and disposition, is so enmeshed in nature that it is clear enough to condemn anyone holding to it. "Unrighteousness," which is the absence of right conduct toward others, points to an anti-moral mind frame and concerns especially unethical deeds committed by man against man, erupting from unrighteous or unjust thinking. Conversely, the basis of acceptable conduct rests on the proper attitude of man toward a merciful God and to his fellow man.

Everyone is to have a basic sense of godliness or God-mindedness. The evidence of a higher power is clearly within reach, both in the creation and the inner sense of ought, the conscience. Therefore, God expects proper behavior from all people; to fail in this or to suppress the truth in the heart is to incur Heaven's wrath. No excuse will be accepted at the future judgment (v. 20).

GOD EVIDENT WITHIN

The teaching of the previous verse is explained in Romans 1:19: "Because that which is known about God is evident within them; for God made it evident to them." The word "because" introduces the reasons why God's wrath is revealed: He has made Himself known (*to gnoston*) in man's conscience and through the creative order. This two-fold general revelation cannot be avoided because of its universality, and the entire human race is accountable to it.

"That which is known of God is manifest in them (*en antois*)" points to the hearts and consciences of everyone (Robertson, 4:328, Wuest, *Word Studies from the Greek New Testament*, Vol. I, [Romans] p. 30). Vincent's *Word Studies in the New Testament* says that the emphasis in the clause should be on the word *in* (3:15). Thus, everyone has a sense of morality which shows in them, written in the heart and reason or conscience.

Knowledge of God also was shown to man in the glorious created universe which testifies to God's everlasting power, goodness, providence, and divinity. The effect of creation demands an adequate Cause to explain it (Acts 14:15-17, 17:26-28; Col. 1:16-17, Heb. 3:3-4). Truth for Jew and Gentile alike begins with these foundational principles of general revelation—that God discloses Himself in nature and in the conscience of all. These twin universal manifestations, clearly understood in the things made and in man's inner sense of right and wrong, are expressed in the Greek aorist indicative tense (Shepard, p. 372), pointing to both continuity of this knowledge and actual occurrences in the case of all individuals throughout history (Hendrickson, pp. 372, 376).

Thus, God's providence has made it abundantly clear what is known concerning Him to all "people and tribes and tongues" (see Rev. 5:9, 7:9). These manifestations of God are not only expressed in the material universe, the macrocosm, but also in man's inner nature, his reason and conscience, the microcosm. Everyone has the knowledge and reality of God revealed to them in each of these ways. These proofs of God are not indefinite or obscure, but all are well within man's capability of being understood. Nature and the broad principles of morality within every person are the teachers about God and the heart or conscience is the student.

James Denney succinctly sums up this two-fold revelation of God to all mankind: "God's power, and the totality of the divine attributes constituting the divine nature, are inevitably impressed upon the mind by nature." Moving from the proof of God through the creation, Denney advances to his second point: "There is [also] that within man which so catches the meaning of all that is without as to issue an instinctive knowledge of God.... This knowledge involves duties, and men are without excuse because, when in possession of it, they did not perform these duties; that is, did not glorify the God whom they thus knew" (cited in Wuest, *Word Studies*, [Romans], p. 20).

Romans 1:18-19 therefore expressly teaches several vital truths about how God has made Himself known to all people everywhere: (1) This revelation is not accomplished through Scripture but exists openly in nature, in history and in conscience, as God actively disclosed Himself through these ways to the created. (2) Man on his own initiative did not discover God; such knowledge engraved upon man's heart is also evident in the creation. (3) More than just covenant Jews and Christians, Gentiles outside of a formal covenant with God also possess these truths. (4) God's wrath will surely come against the impiety of God-rejecting individuals and their lack of conformity to living justly under moral principles and recognition of a specially created universe. These points are amplified throughout the rest of the chapter.

GOD SEEN IN NATURE

In Romans 1:20, the apostle Paul reaches a conclusion: "For since the creation of the world His invisible attributes, His eternal power and divine nature, have been clearly seen, being understood through what has been made, so that they are without excuse."

Since God has made everything self-evident and distinct, and manifests Himself through the creation and a moral consciousness in every man, everyone is thus "without excuse" for not knowing Him, for all men have both this inner and outer knowledge. That which would be known about God has been made plain, self-evident, in the "invisible things" which God has made visible—a true paradox.

God's unwritten general revelation has been made available to man ever since Genesis, and in no way did it begin or end with the prophets and the apostles. Through His everlasting power and divinity, this evidence is clearly perceived by all who would not suppress it (v. 18b). As long as the creation exists and consciences function, mankind has continual unmistakable evidence that a Higher Power exists. This faith-building general revelation is as reliable as revealed Scripture in disclosing the reality of God and His moral principles and rule over nature.

And so, no person can excuse himself for not honoring God, who made him a being who can recognize moral imperatives and who should realize that "right" should be practiced. Nature, the product of creation and not of special prophetic or apostolic revelation, attests to the one true living God of heaven. This explanation is set forth in the most general, abstract form (present tense, passive voice) without any limitation of time or persons (Murray, *Epistle to the Romans*, p. 38).

The teaching of Romans 1:20 should not be minimized. "It is a clear declaration to the effect that the visible creation as God's handiwork makes manifest the invisible perfection of God as its creator..." (Murray, p. 39). The "have been clearly seen" in the passage points to a continual manifestation of the being and perfection of God, as forcefully expressed in Psalm 19:1: "The heavens declare the glory of God."

The evidence of creation is obvious, even in this present day, that God will not excuse anyone who denies His existence, power, and moral order. An ancient wise man recorded, "The fool has said in his heart, there is no God" (Prov. 14:1). Far from developing systematic theology, Paul recordss general concepts are available to all—the people of covenant and Gentile alike—whether living before or after the cross. The never-ending revelation of creation continually makes all men inexcusable before God for not responding to Him in truth and righteousness.

Every person possessing even limited intelligence can understand God's eternal power by what He has made. God's invisible things include His unity, immutability, knowledge, wisdom, and justice. Moses Lard pointed out that "perceived" means "discovered by the senses of the mind" (*Commentary on Romans*, p. 50). Men everywhere can comprehend certain characteristics of God otherwise undiscoverable to them, even apart from special revelation, the Bible.

These traits are called "unseen" or "invisible" because eyes cannot fall upon them. They are understood by the mind only. Such knowledge is preserved in God's creation and in man's inner sense of ought and are discerned through reasoning and searching for truth. Thus, perceiving that God exists is as much a rational process as it is natural. The evidence is "out there," and everyone is obligated to grasp it, using the mental faculties which God has supplied. Man is expected to search for truth, for Jesus said, "Seek and ye shall find, knock and it shall be opened unto you" (Matt. 7:7). See also Chapter Seven.

DISHONORING GOD

R omans 1:21 gives additional reasons for the inexcusableness of the unbelieving Gentiles throughout the world: "For even though they knew God, they did not honor Him as God, or give thanks; but they became futile in the speculations, and their foolish hearts were darkened."

Evidently, Gentiles were fully aware of God and had attained a clear knowledge of Him from the revelation of nature, for He had manifested it to them. Since it was plainly seen (v. 20), it was not based on vague speculation. This knowledge (*gnosko*) means to know by personal experience (W. E. Vine, *Dictionary*, p. 637), through the establishment of a relationship. Throughout the ages, untold numbers of morally upright non-covenant people have sought after God and found His favor.

Yet an even larger delegation of ungrateful Gentiles "did not honor Him as God, nor give thanks" (v. 21), though evidently they all were dependent upon His bountiful care and providence as the source of physical blessings. Through their minds all could realize that God exists, and that He always stands ready to receive all right-thinking men who honestly yearn to have fellowship with the Higher Power. They did not act out of mere ignorance, as did the Athenians of Acts 17:22-34. Rather, they knew precisely that there is only one Creator but willfully bartered that truth for falsehood and idolatry. The creation itself is therefore sufficient to move all people toward a worshipful attitude of a Greater Being, a Superior Presence.

But man also can become futile and vain in their reasoning, and their hearts can darken as they cease to follow various ethical precepts learned. As this begins to happen, God sees to it that such individuals stew in their own juices. He pours forth His wrath upon all who reject Him after they fully have heard and understand the evidence and deny that He is truth and reality.

Verses 22-23 address those who, considering themselves to be sophisticated ones—*suphoi*—are actually just the opposite: "professing to be wise, they became fools, and exchanged the glory of the incorruptible God for an image in the form of corruptible man and of birds and animals and crawling creatures."

And so, the Gentiles' poor spiritual state is the result of a falling away from the original revelation of the Creator-God in His works (see Isa. 24:5). This is knowledge devoid of true wisdom. The result is idolatry (v. 23). How shameful! The true God of heaven had been swapped for images of birds, beasts, and creeping things. In Isaiah 44:9-20, God strongly condemns such practices, putting the idols to rout. All such visual representations of the Higher Power are fatuous, failing by attempting to localize God and reduce Him to man's puny base.

Ancient and modern evolutionary theories in all forms are good examples of man worshiping the creature instead of the Creator. The faithless teacher implants liberal philosophy into students, without regard to reverence for God. R. L. Whiteside comments on the fact that God gives up on such people, allowing them to follow their own ways (*Commentary on Romans*, p. 33). Such thinking closely resembles superstition, which is ignorant reverence. Worshiping idols or other mortals is knowingly and willfully done, and God aggressively condemns such behavior.

The highest truth of all is that the Eternal God the Father is the Creator of everything that is good, and thus He deserves continual service and adoration by His creatures. The lie which is worse than all others is that some created being or idol might represent the Creator, and that it should be worshiped along with or instead of God. Humanism whether ancient or modern perpetuates untruths against God by denial of supernatural creation; it instead venerates mere man as the pinnacle of the cosmic process of evolution.

Verses 24-25, a judicial pronouncement, show that God turns away from all individuals who embrace false wisdom: "Therefore, God gave them over in the lusts of their hearts to impurity, that their bodies might be dishonored among them. For they exchanged the truth of God for a lie, and worshiped and serviced the creature rather than the Creator, who is blessed forever. Amen."

Though restraining men by moral persuasion or other hindrances, God hands sinners over completely to their pernicious ways when He is completely cast off and ungodliness abounds. Sin destroys all whose attitude is geared to transgression, punishing them not through force but in the consequences of the evil deeds they commit.

Moses Lard aptly writes: "God gives people up when He ceases to restrain them from evil or protect them against it..." (*Commentary*, p. 57). Until that moment, people are under His protective care. In this regard, God leaves them alone to do as they please without hindrance from Him, in the matter of sin. God has constant oversight of man's affairs. A denial of an immediate, constant divine providence in human discourse is part of the blindness of verse 21.

God is not indifferent toward us, for the Most High is intimately involved in all nations as well as with every individual. Some say He does not engage in this because nature and "New Testament laws" are fixed and unalterable; but the very idea of an absentee God who wound it all up with special apostolic revelation late in the first century is not taught in Scripture. Evolution, idolatry, and most other modern philosophies are surely instances of "exchanging the truth of God for a lie" (Romans 1:25). Men swapped the realities of the Creator God and His protective care for mythology and images. These people had the truth (*aletheian*). They could not trade away what they did not possess. Indeed, the Gentiles knew what was right concerning God.

A CATALOG OF EVIL DEEDS

That ungodly men tested God and cast Him aside is shown in Romans 1:26-27: "For this reason God gave them over to degrading passions; for their women exchanged the natural function for that which is unnatural, and in the same way also the men abandoned the natural function of the woman and burned in their desire toward one another, men with men committing indecent acts and receiving in their own person the due penalty of their error."

As explained by R. C. H. Lenski, "They [non truth-seeking men] did not let their *gnosis* of God produce *epignosis*. They did not permit the natural intellectual 'knowledge' which was thrust upon them to yield the permanent possession (*echein*) of fuller inner 'realization' so as to control their hearts and lives" (*Commentary on Romans*, p.118). The shameful consequence: God cast them aside, fully relinquished them (v. 24).

The wrath of verse 18 is extended to its logical limit in verses 28-32. "In this paragraph we see the floodgates opened wide, and the frightful torrent engulfing the ungodly" (Lenski, p. 117). They filled themselves to the brim with moral and spiritual decadence. God gives people over to their own sins when the cup of iniquity is full, as with the Amorites (Gen. 15:16). Only then does God bring full judgment, for they are no longer fit to exist.

The evildoers in verses 26-31 "know the ordinance of God" (v. 32), indicating the adequacy of general revelation in nature. As stated by R. L. Whiteside, "But how did they know that these sins and that those who practiced them were worthy of death? There is embedded in man's nature a consciousness of right and wrong. If he never had a [special] revelation from God, he knows that it is wrong to abuse his body and to mistreat his fellows...A [special] revelation from God was never intended to create new faculties in man. It does not plant in the human heart a consciousness of right and wrong, but [special revelation] does guide and refine that consciousness, and places motives before man, to induce him to do right" (*Commentary on Romans*, p. 97).

American Restoration pioneers such as J. W. McGarvey, Philip Pendleton, Moses Lard, and even Whiteside in their various commentaries open up the possibility that Gentiles knew good and evil because of earlier special revelation to Noah and others which had been passed down by oral and written tradition. This notion is not expressed specifically in the text of Romans 1:18-31, which clearly states that the creation itself together with the conscience are adequate revelations from heaven to account for the state of righteousness or sin in which people find themselves. Through Natural Law, men may see God's divine blessing, but also might experience His wrath.

Various patriarchs did pass down orally various revelations from their source from father to son, even as righteous Abraham did (Gen. 18:19). Ancestral knowledge of God may have originated from the time of Adam and Eve (Gen. 2-3) but especially from Noah, in the post-flood era (Gen. 9:1-28). The logical presumption is that these truths (sometimes called the Noahic code) were forwarded and preserved in oral tradition, now lost forever.

Still, the star witnesses and evidence of God and His law of nature is the magnificent creation together with man's inner sense of ought; his sober reasoning upon these things and relationships with other people are the sources of his moral knowledge—that which many had traded for idolatry and lasciviousness (Rom. 1:25). These abominations are both the cause (v. 18) and punitive consequences (vv. 24, 26, 28) of their godlessness. While casting off God from their mental comprehension and realization (*epignosi*—v. 28), these men failed to rid themselves of realizing (*epignosis*, in participle form) the just or righteous decree of God (v. 32).

When Paul convicted Gentiles of sin in Romans 1, he did not appeal to prophetic or apostolic special revelation, Scripture. The Ten Commandments and other Bible texts are not needed to show that adultery, stealing, lying, etc. are wrong. Through Natural Law an awareness of these a moral transgressions is embedded in the human conscience. Though men do what they will or choose to fight it, this knowledge clings to them, not merely in their *gnosis* (knowledge) but in their *epignosis* (clear, fuller comprehension) because man is a moral creature (see Lenski, *Commentary on Romans*, p. 156). There is a constant war in the flesh and good impulses battle bad ones. People are accountable to truths only as exposed to them in *epignosis*.

All evil men thus convicted are worthy of spiritual death (v. 32). And so, everyone should recognize that in their *epignosis* of God they ought to give thanks (v. 21) and live in keeping with the knowledge of right and wrong they have, in godliness and righteousness (expressed in the negative in verse 18). And so, when anyone violates this sense of ought, he knows that such is contrary to the will of the Divine Nature, and his conscience accuses him of the sober reality that his relationship with God is very much amiss.

Worship of objects other than the true and living God condemned. (Acts 17:29)

CHAPTER THREE

◇◇◇◇◇◇◇◇◇◇◇◇◇◇

NATURAL LAW
IN ANCIENT SOURCES

A s God disclosed His mind and will through Natural Law to everyone throughout time, He has blessed the righteous with redemption, priesthood, excused consciences and present acceptance which is salvation. A review of both the Old and New Testaments will show that these blessings are not the exclusive domain of ancient Jews and Christians, the people of the covenant, but are worldwide, universal. Anyone at any time can make moral decisions under a Natural Law standard and enjoy acceptance by God.

JEWISH SCRIPTURES

G enesis 2:18, 23-24 states that "...It is not good for man to be alone... Therefore a man leaves his father and his mother and cleaves to his wife, and they become one flesh." Thus, God indicates it is natural for a man to choose a woman for a mate, instead of another man or a beast. God built into mankind a strong physical attraction between the sexes. Though Matthew, Mark and Paul all cite verse 24 to support monogamous marriage, this was not the initial understanding because of the uncensored polygamy among Abraham, David, and many other faithful of Israel. Though never God's ideal, polygamy is not immoral or unnatural (the polygamist sustains a one-flesh relationship with each of his wives, even as when a man joins himself with a prostitute—I Cor. 6:16).

God's first-ever command, the dominion mandate of Genesis 1:28 "to be fruitful and multiply," applies universally to all people, and has never been withdrawn. God even expanded it to Noah after the flood (Gen. 9:1-29), repeating the identical command. This verse expresses a universal function, populating the earth, while Genesis 2:18 shows a natural function, mating. The passages which follow add moral features to these, thus showing the absolute existence of Natural Law, strongly undergirded by saving justice.

Genesis 3:22, "...man has become like one of us knowing good and evil..." teaches that everyone has the capacity to make moral distinctions and then act upon them. What law was then extant other than Natural Law? In Genesis 4:7 God said to Cain, "If you do not well, sin crouches at the door," hungry to see you. Then, after murdering Abel, Cain declared, "...whosoever finds me will slay me..." (v. 14), showing that he was subject to a moral standard.

Fearing for his life, Cain realized that his peers would recognize the heinousness of his crime, thus showing that all of these people lived under the guidance of universal morality. Sin would thus be imputed to Cain, a murderer who was evil, full of jealousy, envy, wrath and lies (I John 3:11-12). On the other hand, Abel was accepted of God because he did what was correct in his heart, and God had regard for that, and this disposition triumphs the specific type of sacrifice he offered.

The prophet Enoch (Gen. 5:21-24) issued warnings to "ungodly sinners," promising eternal judgment upon the wicked (Jude 14). Even in these few examples, various transgressions had been committed, pointing to the existence of a natural order embracing both the good and evil.

Noah's contemporaries severely violated God's order of creation, living by brute strength and contriving wicked schemes contrary to morality (Gen. 6). The expression "All flesh had corrupted their way upon earth..." (v. 12) shows that man had a definite right way in which to walk, a moral standard; wholesale departure from it through lawlessness and disobedience (I Pet. 3:20) brought God's spiritual judgment and the earth's destruction by a universal flood. This is what Noah taught in his generation.

As sin reigned at Sodom and Gomorrah primarily through idolatry and homosexuality, universal moral law was violated (Gen. 13:10-14:12). These people had lived an ungodly lascivious lifestyle contrary to nature, but righteous Lot was troubled by all that he saw. He was delivered from destruction (II Pet. 2:6-8) which presupposes a divine standard of behavior which is either upheld by righteous living or transgressed by wicked people destined for eternal punishment (Jude 7). Finding a sufficient number of morally conscientious people in those cities would have averted their destruction.

In about 2100 B.C. Abraham, a God-conscious man fully justified by faith, walked perfectly before the Lord (Gen. 17:1). This suggests a moral standard, inasmuch as he did righteousness and justice (Gen. 18:19). As the father of the faithful (Gen. 14:18, Heb. 11:8), Abraham kept God's "commandments, statutes and laws" (Gen. 26:5) relating to ethics, right-living and principles of a proper relationship with God under Natural Law. He was doing the truth long before anything was written down as Scripture for the benefit of God's later covenant people.

This general but often specific moral law is what Isaiah later had in mind when he mentioned a universally applicable covenant (24:5) to the "world"—people of all nations throughout time failing to follow their available light. Isaiah said, "The people have disobeyed the laws and violated the statutes, broken the everlasting covenant"—all developed long ago in Genesis. God further disclosed heavenly revelation which had been displayed by Abraham to later Jewish prophets, together with ceremonial, dietary and civil law.

Contemporary with Abraham was God-fearing Melchizedek, a king of righteousness at Salem, and a type of Christ. Though not benefiting from a specific formal covenant with God and thus did not have access to written special revelation, he nevertheless was called "a priest of God Most High" (Gen. 14:18), serving the same true spirit Being whom Abraham worshiped, even in the midst of a wicked society notorious for sexual immorality. In a pagan culture, he united kingship and priesthood with acceptable service to God.

Genesis 14:17-24 records Abraham's remarkable encounter with this grand man of faith and venerator of the true God. While Abraham had entered into a formal eternal covenant with Yahweh (Gen. 15:1-18, 17:4-7), the priestly king in holiness served El Elyon, the Canaanite name for the same Creator God known to Abraham. Melchizedek's name for God also appears in ancient Phoenician texts, and the name El became integrated into the Hebrew tongue in such words as El Shaddai (Gen. 17:1), "El" compounds as in El Bethel, and in the familiar Elohim. Abraham and Melchizedek were thus spiritual brothers in El Elyon/Yahweh, standing side by side in the cause of righteousness, with no hint of rivalry or jealousy between them.

Melchizedek expressed religious fellowship with Abraham by offering him a common meal of bread and wine and blessing him as a deliverer from heathen enemies through invoking the non-covenant name, El Elyon. Scripture records nothing negative about the Gentile priest; Abraham gave him a tenth of warfare spoils he had recently gained, an act which in New Testament times triggered the author of the Hebrew epistle to comment extensively upon Melchizedek's greatness (7:1-25).

Even King David realized that the Anointed One to come, the king and priest of Israel, would not have membership in the temporal restricted lineage of the Jewish Levitical priesthood of special revelation, but rather the Christ would be a priest emanating from Natural Law, "after the order of Melchizedek" (Psa. 110:4). It is eternal in duration and confirmed by a divine oath (Heb. 7:3). Like the general revelation which Melchizedek was subject to, always "just there" with no beginning or ending, Jesus' priesthood was founded on the basis of power flowing from a life that cannot end (vv. 16-17). Melchizedek's office served as the prototype of the unique worldwide priesthood of Jesus Christ.

In addition to holding a superior priesthood, Melchizedek also had the grace to bless even the mighty Abraham (Heb. 7:7). Melchizedek rightly possessed the titles of priest and king because he served a good number of authentic faithful God worshipers. This line of morally focused God-fearers was entirely independent of the covenant line of God's people beginning with Abraham.

Evidently, God provided Melchizedek's called out assembly with a general revelation of Himself in the conscience of all. He might have learned about God directly in private revelations lost to history. Or knowledge of Him could have been handed down orally from his ancestors in the post-flood era. Truths which God gave directly to Adam and Eve (Gen. 3) and to Noah (6:13-7:5, 8:15-17, 9:1-8) probably came down to the generation of Melchizedek through faithfully preserved oral tradition. In any of these ways he came to know the one monotheistic God of heaven, and learned the truth about Him, addressing the eternal Creator by a name other than Yahweh.

Also exerting moral influence in the Gentile world apart from the special revelation of written law was Jethro, a priest of Midian and a believer in God (Exod. 18:1-12, 2:16, 3:1). His standard was general revelation with the moral law in the heart. Further, Jethro gave instruction to Moses (Exod. 18:13-27), offering sacrifices to God with the covenant ones, Aaron and Moses and other elders of Israel joining him (v. 12). This priest of God had knowledge of God which was entirely independent of anything disclosed to Moses, for it was given to him prior to the revelation at Mt. Sinai.

One document outside of Israel's prophetic line is the book of Job, though its hero is the God of Abraham, Isaac, and Jacob. While fending off accusers, Job defended his morality, for he had not denied the words of the Holy One and did not rebel against His decrees (Job 6:10). He had not turned aside from commandments which flowed from God's lips but instead cherished them (23:11-12). And so he could boast of a Defender: "I know that my redeemer lives!" (19:25).

Job had knowledge of God's will through unpreserved primeval disclosures of God's ways long before Moses promulgated commandments to Israel. Thus, Job gained redemption and acceptance under Natural Law through the creation (see Job 38:1-42:6). He rationally defended his actions in terms of general universal law of nature, and not because of specially revealed precepts and duties, such as those promulgated by the prophets God later sent to Israel and Judah.

The righteous Hebrew Joseph (Gen. 39-42) knew right and wrong before God. On one occasion, Potiphar's wife grabbed Joseph by the sleeve, demanding that he sleep with her. Joseph tore himself away, leaving his jacket behind (39:12-

17). How did Joseph know of the sin of adultery? Evidently his heart embraced a moral standard, wherein actions are either inherently right or wrong, as taught both by his father Jacob and through a moral awareness given to all by God. Similarly, Abimilech of the Philistines knew that he would be sinning against the Creator if he engaged in adultery, learning this from a message from Israel's God (Gen. 20:1-18).

Balaam, a Gentile prophet out of Mesopotamia—regarded by Peter and John as a compromiser and archetype of false teachers in the Christian age (II Pet. 2:15, Rev. 2:14)—nevertheless received revelations from God (Num. 23:5-16), possessing heavenly knowledge apart from specially revealed written law. Much later from that same region and without hearing any of God's prophets, Babylon's arrogant king Nebuchadnezzar praised and honored the King of heaven, whose works he saw as truth (Dan. 4:35-37). Another pagan idolater, Artaxerxes of Persia, also acknowledged apart from the written Law of Moses that the true God resided in heaven (Ezra 7:12-24). Darius the Mede (Ezra 6:12-15) echoed this truth.

Other pagans who received heavenly revelations which led them to recognize the God of Israel were king Hyram of Tyre (II Chron. 2:11-12), Pharoah-Neco of Egypt (II Chron. 35:20-21), and Cyrus, who learned that the God of heaven charged him to assist covenanted Jews in rebuilding the temple in Jerusalem (II Chron. 36:22-23; cf. Ezra 1:1-2). King Darius admonished the people to "tremble with fear before the God of Daniel" (Dan. 6:26-28).

Amos wrote oracles against various heathen nations, each of which could offer no excuse for barbarism (1:3-2:16). All of them should have known better than to plunder, rape, and violate human rights. Because they engaged in these things, God accused these people of "transgression," the violation of the universal moral order. God sent the prophet Jonah to the great heathen city of Ninevah because of the peoples' wickedness; some of them subsequently repented and turned from evil ways (Jonah 3:5-10, Luke 11:29-32) and turned to Israel's God. To this list can be added Rahab (Josh. 2:11, Jas. 2:25), Ruth (Ruth 1:16-17), and an Ethiopian eunuch, Ebed-malech (Jer. 39:15-18), each of whom trusted in the one true God and received blessings.

The preacher of Ecclesiastes emphasized the predetermined character of earthly events as a means to show that nature cannot be altered from its majestic, inexorable course. In this structure is revealed good and evil, as in 7:14 and in the statements in verses 15 and 17: "Be not righteous to excess...be not wicked to excess..." Everyone must live in accordance with the moral order in a world where these choices are constantly present.

The prophet Isaiah compared sinful covenant people under Moses with ancient non-covenanters worthy of destruction. "Except Yahweh of hosts had left unto us a very small remnant, we should have been as Sodom, we should have been like unto Gomorrah" (1:9). Those lascivious people were without excuse, as were some of Isaiah's contemporaries, who would have been entirely wiped out, except that the Lord stepped in to save a moral remnant.

Isaiah in chapters 13-23 addressed the polluted earth, eleven foreign nations round about Israel, affirming that "the world," would experience judgment because "they have transgressed the law, violated the statutes, and broken the everlasting covenant" (24:5). Because of sin these peoples had defiled and desecrated God's moral order. This "covenant," an expression coextensive with the transgressed laws and statutes, has been made with all of the human race, and when violated judgment overtakes the entire world.

This covenant dates from the time of Noah (Gen. 9:16), and even before, and points to a moral order in creation with fundamental understanding of God's expectations for human conduct, right behavior. Jonah, Elijah, Elisha, and other prophets of God also offered instruction to Gentile nations, showing that there is a universal fundamental understanding of God's expectation for upright behavior under an eternal order of right and wrong (see Chapter Ten).

Evidently, there is general moral discourse among all people a desire to know a standard of right and wrong which, when violated, brings forth God's wrath (Rom. 1:18). In the midst of much evil and corruption, Noah and other upright people walked with God (Gen. 6:9), finding favor in Him by living according to the divine moral law, God's universal truths and principles of righteousness.

CREATION PSALMS

The reality of the one true spirit God and His mighty works, apart from special prophetic and apostolic revelation, is taught through various creation psalms. Influenced by the obvious empirical truths of Natural Law, these poets meditated upon God's glorious handiwork, showing that His wisdom and creative power is mingled with moral goodness. Their work does not unfold a system of theology or a doctrinal network—that was not their purpose—but instead the writings mirror the thoughts and emotions of God-fearing poets of Israel before the presence of their great and glorious Maker.

In picturing the creation, each of these Psalms shows that God fully controls the universe. "How awesome are thy works! All of the earth bows down before you" was the psalmist's proper response toward such a truth, expressing this reality with deep feeling and rich imagination (66:3-4). The entire of Psalm 104 displays the Creator's greatness, majesty, and splendor which are seen as He erected the heavens and established land and sea, vegetation, and the sun and the moon. Indeed, in wisdom and mighty power, God made the bountiful earth and the living things upon it, all of which testify to intricate beauty and purposeful design.

When considering nature and the mighty creative works of this glorious One, every person has a capacity to honor and serve Him acceptably and morally. By contemplating these things, anyone can acquire simple, authentic faith in a fair and just God. It can lead to a covenant in principle with Heaven (see Chapter Five). God never refuses the heartfelt, sincere response or worship from anyone who truly loves Him. And, as the ancients sang the praises of the great Creator God, they perhaps implicitly embraced the reality of His son as well, for whom the creation was made (Col. 1:17).

David's 8th Psalm notes that God's name is uniformly majestic "in all the world." While pondering the seemingly eternal moon and the stars scattered throughout the heavens, the psalmist wondered why the all-powerful Giver of life would have concerned Himself with mere mortals (v. 4, cp. Psa. 89:36-37). But the superlative Creator generally invests every person with a degree of dignity just below His own, giving man dominion over all earthly things. This is universal general revelation for all people.

On another occasion, the same psalmist contemplated all of nature's activities and concluded that God deserved our continual worship and glory and strength (29:1-12). His testimonies were utterly to be trusted, and could be fully relied upon, for His strength should be evident to everyone. Psalms 93, 95, and 97 declare that the King of all things is the One who deserves unqualified, universal praise, for God has through nature shown His absolute rule over all realms. As universal monarch, He is worthy of our service.

To all who realize that they are wonderfully made (Psa. 139:4), the God who wove them together (v. 13) takes note of this measure of faith but does not delight in human sturdiness (147:10). The poet of Psalm 148 called for everyone to praise God for His mighty works, in the unified heavens and on the earth. In these things the Creator is clearly seen, and so man's proper response from the farthest corners of the earth is to stand in awe of thy works (33:8-9). To the honest heart, the evidence of God is in the things made, the magnificent creation.

In Psalm 19, David said that the heavens continuously manifest the glory of God (v.1); they are a marvelous display of His craftsmanship. Throughout the day and night the heavenly bodies keep on communicating the reality of the creation, bubbling forth information about God. Seemingly without a sound or a word, silent in the skies, their message reaches worldwide. "There is no speech, nor are there words, where their voice is not heard" (v. 4). Compare these words with Romans 1:19, a verse which states the creation of the world is clearly evident in the things made (see Chapter Two).

The book of Genesis also rests its case on the postulate that the created surely should be able to recognize nature's grandeur. For man, this calls for godliness and a reverential attitude toward God, who in turn seeks responsible behavior through respect for the moral living and His creation. Nobody should willfully ignore universal truth. Everyone in all of the ages is obligated to honor the Creator; His pure, eternal, just moral principles serve as the basis for salvation and judgment of everyone at the end of time.

Though God has revealed Himself to one and all generally in nature and in the conscience of all, He sent prophets to specially reveal His will to Israel and to apostles and teachers to instruct disciples of Christ. Everyone is without excuse for not acknowledging the Creator as God. From observation and the eye of understanding and reason, non-Christians can learn about God's glory, power, benevolence, wisdom, orderliness, etc. God's wrath will fall upon all who do not honor Him as this world's Sustainer and Governor.

This general standard of ethics in moral law, fully contemplated spiritually by the mind, has existed ever since Adam. Cain killed Abel and he knew it was wrong; Lamech murdered and it was wrong. The thoughts and actions of Noah's contemporaries contrived wicked schemes continually (Gen. 6:5); they were subject to the same universal standard as the people of Sodom and Gomorrah, whom God destroyed because of "grievous sins" (18:20).

All of these individuals were instructed by Natural Law, as were the various nations of Canaan, whom God judged evil and abominable (Deut. 18:9-14). The men of Nineveh, in need of repentance at the time of Jonah, were amenable to this unwritten standard as well; the great nation of Babylon was similarly subject to punishment for evil deeds. A general awareness of moral living is embedded in the very nature of man, giving him a general consciousness of right and wrong. Even when God gave the Ten Commandments and other ethical laws to Israel, He did not arbitrarily declare that certain acts were sinful, because from earliest times many acts of men were intrinsically unacceptable in heaven on the basis of moral law.

JEWISH AND GRECIAN WRITINGS

Various writings of the Jewish apocrypha and pseudepigrapha, religious works that never were canonized as part of the Old Testament, contain numerous references to themes of Natural Law. Among the most forceful are concepts from the *Testament of Judah*, written in about 100 B.C. The writer spoke of a spirit of truth and a spirit of deceit; between them is a spirit of understanding of the mind, which can incline itself in either direction (20:1-2). Either of these is "written on the hearts of men" (v. 3). The spirit of truth "testifies all things and accuses all, and the sinner is burnt up [by his own heart] and cannot raise his face to the judge" (v. 5).

There are obvious striking parallels of this statement with Paul's words in

Romans 2:15. Good and evil and law requirements are written in men's hearts. Paul's appeal to the conscience, excusing and accusing thoughts, equates with the "understanding of the mind (*syneidesis*)," the faculty which leads a man to choose either truth or deceit. Both passages also make reference to a judgment. These similarities are no mere coincidence; Paul conceivably could have had a copy of the *Testament of Judah* before him when he wrote the book of Romans.

The Jewish *Talmud* often speaks of two urges within every person, one toward evil and the other toward goodness, each of which is ever present (see Chapter Ten). The wicked are under control of their evil impulse, but the righteous have their heart in submission to the good. The mighty before God are those who conquer inordinate desires. Thus, within the breast of every man are two spirits vying with each other. The heart wrestles with these principles, and makes choices as to which spirit will prevail in his life, a constant struggle even for the apostle Paul (Rom. 7:14-25).

There is a war in the flesh and good impulses battle the bad, which is "king" over all limbs and organs. But continual violation of the conscience sears it, rendering it ineffective in the struggle. According to *IV Maccabees*, all these emotions are divinely implanted in mankind (2:21) and are therefore ineradicable (1:6; 3:2, 5). God gave a law to the mind, the medium of the senses, and in living by conscience and thus available light, one may maintain a temperate, just, good, and exemplary reign (2:22-23).

In teaching Greeks in the fifth century B.C. pagan world, Socrates declared that he had found the true God in his own moral consciousness. This conviction was confirmed by the eye of moral understanding and the universe's orderly nature (Rom. 1:19). Socrates also uplifted the power of reason, and had full confidence in human nature, acknowledging that God had placed general universality of morality deep within man's consciousness. He upheld self-examination as echoed by the apostle Paul to test self to see if you are in the faith (II Cor. 13:5), while holding in deep disdain willful ignorance, prejudice, pretense, and hypocrisy. Such amazing moral insights as these may have helped prepare the Grecian mind for Paul's later preaching about Christ to them (Acts 16:11-18:17).

Rome's great political orator and philosopher, Cicero, defined Natural Law with remarkable economy, in about 50 B.C.: "This law of nature, being co-eval with mankind and dictated by God himself, is of course superior in obligation to any other. It is binding over all the globe, and all countries, and at all times: no human laws are of any validity, if contrary to this; and such of them as are valid derive all their force, and all their authority, mediately or immediately from this original."

THE TEACHING OF JESUS CHRIST

Appeals in Jesus' discourses to a sense of ought and a recognition of the Creator fit well in the mainstream of universal Natural Law. Significantly, Christ's moral teaching strengthens and reinforces this unwritten standard to perfection, providing the ultimate revelation of truth. In the Sermon on the Mount (Matt. 5-7), the Master said that adultery is the logical extension of lust, murder consummates hate and anger, the breaking of vows including agreements and contracts shows a lack of integrity (a form of lying), and the godly response to retaliation is not to resist the evil. He emphasized the loving of enemies, instead of hating them. Jesus ever stressed good behavior and the shunning of evil deeds.

Among Jesus' sayings which are undergirded by moral law include Matthew 5:45, which recognizes that God makes the sun to rise on both the upright and evil people, and sends the elements upon the just and unjust. From his treasure, the good man brings forth good, while the evil man renders bad deeds (Matt. 12:35). At the future judgment, angels will separate the evil from the righteous (Matt. 13:49). On one occasion Jesus pointedly asked, "Is it permitted on the Sabbath to do good or to do harm?" (Mark 3:4). Matthew 7:9-11 recognizes a distinction between a good man who would give someone a loaf instead of a serpent, and the evil man, who is not capable of giving good gifts to his children.

The gospel of Matthew's recurring contrast between good and evil, the sensible and the stupid as in 7:24-27, 10:39, 12:35, 13:41-43, 21:28-32, etc., are universal moral truths which had been evident to man long before they were set forth in Scripture. Concepts like just, right, unjust, and wrong never need special legal disclosure or a revelation from God to be properly understood. The teachings of Jesus show continuity in relations between Israel and the nations by appealing to a general order of right and wrong which is deeply rooted in humanity.

Various other statements by Jesus show that non-Jewish people of His day possessed enough moral and spiritual discernment to justify a positive standing before God, either acceptable or condemnable based upon their deeds. Jesus pronounced woes upon covenant people in Capernaum, Chorazin, and Bethsaida, because of their closed mindedness, their lack of faith in acknowledging his miracles, while simultaneously assuring that people living in the Gentile towns of Tyre and Sidon would have repented upon seeing the same mighty works (Matt. 11:20-24).

And so, because their hearts were in accord with moral principles, many people in those non-Jewish communities possessed the ability to recognize good and evil. Jesus' conclusion that it will be more tolerable for those Gentiles in the judgment indicates that an undetermined number of them will yet be saved (v. 22). In another context, the Lord made the same argument for certain ones living in the sinful cities of Sodom and Gomorrah (Matt. 10:15).

Jesus encouraged many among the covenant Jews to learn from Gentiles, by following their examples of faith. In Matthew 12:41, Jesus declared that righteous men of Ninevah would rise at the final judgment with the generation of Jesus and condemn it, for those Gentiles had repented at Jonah's word, and a greater one was now among them. Though under a formal covenant with God, the Jews with whom Jesus came in contact did not recognize what was the superior mission.

In an earlier period of Israel, Elijah and Elisha considered good people in surrounding nations targets of favor, and those people were just as worthy as those living in the home country. A widow at Zarephath in Sidon was held in high regard, over and above other widows among the Jews (Luke 4:25-27). Jesus took note of her faith, made even more remarkable because she lived amid the idolatry of Baal (I Kgs. 16:31-33). Jesus also commended Naaman the Syrian, who was healed by Elisha (vv. 4:28-29); the Lord's synagogue audience in Nazareth took exception to the implied contrast between that favored man and their lack of faith (Luke 4:25-30).

A certain Roman centurion's belief in God was greater than anyone else's throughout Israel (Luke 7:1-10), and Jesus showed amazement. There was also the great trust of a Canaanite woman in Tyre and Sidon who sought out Jesus to cure her demonized daughter (Matt. 15:21-28). And so, in Jesus' day, Gentiles who practiced positive moral living also experienced God's blessings, as did faithful Jews in Jesus' day, people secure in covenant with God.

These incidents are in full accord with Jesus' words in John 3:20-21, "For everyone who does evil hates the light, and does not come to the light...but he who practices the truth comes to the light..." Some truth and therefore a measure of accountability is a universal phenomenon, and doers of right continually accept additional truth and do not willfully reject it. With an opportunity to hear the gospel, responsible people receive Jesus in the gospel, the ultimate and fullest expression of light. Evil people whose deeds would be exposed by that same light, choose to cast aside God's truth.

Luke 12:47 tells of two groups who were worthy of strokes of the lash at the final judgment. Knowledgeable but disobedient servants would be treated more sternly than the ignorant and the disobedient (see Chapter Eleven). Jesus then added significantly, "And to whomever much is given, of him shall much be required; and to whom they commit much, of him the more will be expected" (v. 48b, Matt. 13:12). In a parallel passage, John 9:39-41, Jesus equated being blind or lacking truth with having no guilt or sin. Gentiles under a natural moral standard are judged only by what truths are available to them, i.e., what revelation of God they know and comprehend. Hearers of the message who decide to reject God's truths—whether general or specially revealed—stand condemned (John 12:48, II Thess. 1:8; see also I Pet. 4:17).

With this distinction in mind Jesus later said, "If I had not come and spoken to them, they would not have had sin, but now they have no excuse for their sin" (John 15:22-24). Natural Law will be the standard of judgment. Others who heard Jesus preach and witnessed his good deeds and then refused the teaching, had additional accountability. Thereafter, they were in sin for rejecting the teaching, and not before.

In Matthew 19:1-9, Jesus appealed to the creative natural order to instruct his people on the permanence of marriage, that God made male and female from the beginning (vv. 4, 8). Although Jesus clearly advocated a return to what was in the time of Moses and before, he also allowed for hardness of heart back then and even today in the matter of divorce, principally because of the exceptive clause of verse 9. In this celebrated call to repentance, Jesus taught that everyone should naturally follow what was right in the matter of faithful marriages and not to divorce, which is an unnatural act against another.

Thus, Jesus' words concerning marriage deserve no retroactive application to the time of Moses and the prophets, for Jesus is providing information exclusively for Christians. The passage does not fit into the Genesis world with its absence of sin and death, so reference to that time would be anachronistic. Matthew 19:9 is best understood when Natural Law's principle of accountability is taken into account: if this teaching *applied* to people before the cross or non-covenanters living at any time, its truths should have been *supplied* to them.

THE BOOK OF ACTS; PETER AND PAUL

On his first missionary journey, Paul told pagans in Galatia that "in bygone days God permitted the nations to go their own way, but He never left Himself without witness" (Acts 14:15-17). Reminders of the Creator abound in the rain, good crops, and the food eaten, for God had made the heaven, earth, sea, and all that is in them. These truths coupled with Romans 1 adequately show that God has revealed Himself *generally* to all people through the creation and human nature, and *specially* to prophets and apostles for the benefit of covenant people. Later, after Paul had landed on Grecian soil, Paul declared to the Athenians that God had made the world and all things in it (Acts 17:24).

Evidently, any one can recognize as good what God by nature declares to be good. Peter taught that all men have the capacity for sound moral judgment, and can discern between good and evil: "Maintain good conduct among the Gentiles, so that, in case they speak against you as wrongdoers, they may see the moral lives you lead...Keep your conscience clear so that, when you are abused, those who revile your good behavior might be put to shame" (I Peter 2:12,

3:16). Jesus himself also sought a determination of what is proper by asking, "Why do you judge for yourselves what is right?" (Luke 12:57).

Besides the text of Romans 1:18-31, commented upon extensively upon in Chapter Two, Paul made other references to Natural Law by appealing directly to nature as a source of guidance for behavior for everybody. Paul admonished the saints to "do what is noble in the sight of all" (Rom. 12:17), and this verse points to sin against the natural order (cp. Rom. 1:26). The apostles olive tree illustration tells of grafting, "contrary to nature," the created order of things (Rom. 11:16-24).

The godless do not distinguish between good and evil (I Thess 4:5; cp. Rom 14:16, 15:14, 16:19). II Timothy 3:2-9 speaks of a heartless, intractable class of people "without natural affection" (v. 3). In that context, the word "natural" points to the very general universal standard which should have been followed from the heart. In another context, Paul declared that "nature teaches..." which might be a custom or long held practice (I Cor. 11:14; cp. Eph. 2:3).

EARLY CHRISTIAN WRITINGS

Recognition that moral law underlies God's dealing with man has a long history in Christian apologetics. In about 165 A.D., Justin Martyr in his *Dialogue with Trypho* wrote about "...those who do that which is universally, naturally, and eternally good are pleasing to God [and] shall be saved through this Christ equally with those righteous men who went before, namely, Noah and Enoch and Jacob, and whoever else there be..." (Ch. 45).

Eusebius, in *Preparation for the Gospel* (VII, 1-12), also recognized this positive moral sense, as did Justin Martyr in another context, who saw in Jesus' teaching an ethic in continuity with Judaism's highest aspirations, but without the shackles of ceremonial rules among which the Jews alone participated (*Dialogue*, Ch.14).

In *Against Heresies* (IV:13.1), Irenaeus in about the year 180 forcefully stated that Christ did not nullify the natural precepts of Moses' law, but rather renewed and enlarged upon them: "and that the Lord did not abrogate the natural [precepts] of the law, by which man is justified, which also those who were justified by faith, and who pleased God, did observe previous to the giving of the law, but that He extended and fulfilled them, is shown from His word [then quoting Matthew 5:20, 21-22, 27-28, 33 etc.]." In IV:13:5, Irenaeus also stated that Christ "has increased and widened those laws which are natural, and noble, and common to all, granting to men...to know God the Father...."

Much later, Thomas Aquinas made a clear distinction between God's supernatural revelations to Israel and the first century saints and Natural Law discerned by conscience. In formulating the latter, he echoed Cicero by saying, "An unjust law is a human law that is not rooted in external law and natural law.

Any law that uplifts human personality is just. Any law that degrades human personality is unjust."

These perspectives found their way into the preaching and writing of the 18th and 19th century Restoration Movement of England and America, by way of philosophers Richard Hooker and also John Locke, who said that information originates in the perception of our senses, our "natural faculties." R. L. Whiteside stated that "There is embedded in man's nature a consciousness of right and wrong." The doctrine of available light specifically addresses these emotions which are divinely implanted in mankind and are ineradicable.

Alexander Campbell said that the two great commands, "Thou shalt love the lord thy God with all thy heart, soul, mind, and strength, and thy neighbor as thyself," are of universal immutable obligation. They belong to the fundamentals of law written in every human heart, serving as the foundation for both the moral aspects of the Law of Moses and Christ's teachings. Campbell saw in Natural Law a moral order or sense for the entire human race, noting that the two great commandments—loving God and neighbor—are universally binding not because they are recorded in the Bible, but because they are inherently right and each human conscience must answer to them. They are the sum and substance of moral law.

Thomas Jefferson rephrased these great moral principles when he said, "We hold these truths to be self-evident, that all men are created equal; that they are endowed by their Creator with certain inalienable rights; that among these are life, liberty and the pursuit of happiness." To Jefferson, self-evident meant sacred and undeniable, obvious; equal was the same as dependent; inalienable also carried the idea of inherent, uncancelable. Most of the nation's founders were steeped in Natural law concepts in their political discourse.

In his "Letter from Birmingham Jail," Martin Luther King demonstrated Natural Law by saying, "One has not only a legal but a moral responsibility to obey just laws. Conversely, one has a moral responsibility to disobey unjust laws. I would agree with St. Augustine that 'an unjust law is no law at all'...A just law is a man-made code that squares with the...law of God. An unjust law is a code that is out of harmony with the moral law..." [then quoting Thomas Aquinas as above].

Therefore, certain God-given things are innate, undeniable, self-evident, ever "in your face." On the testimony of the creation and man's inner spirit, British scientist and Restoration pioneer Michael Faraday concluded that there is a natural moral order. His faith in it was total, so unquestioning that the idea of proving what was obvious seemed absurd to him. A moral sense in the conscience is as much a part of man as his limbs or torso, according to Faraday.

THE VOICES OF WRITERS AND POETS

Like the humorist Mark Twain, who said that the undevout astronomer must be mad, Albert Einstein doubted that there are any disbelieving scientists. In *The World As I See It,* Einstein saw among his colleagues "a religious feeling which took the form of rapturous amazement at the harmony of natural law." It reduces man's puny theological patterns to insignificance.

Philosopher Immanuel Kant declared that the vast starry firmament above, and the general sense of morality within man, filled him with awe (compare with Rom. 1:19). Thus, it would be inconsistent for anyone to be "rapturously amazed" and not be reverent and virtuous, and conscientiously choose the good part.

Thomas Merton taught that every place on the earth shows intelligence and design: "There is not a flower that opens, not a seed that falls into the ground, and not an ear of wheat that nods on the end of its stalk in the wind that does not preach and proclaim the greatness and the mercy of God to the whole world." Ralph Waldo Emerson succinctly stated that "Nature is saturated with Deity." Elizabeth Barrett Browning wrote, "Earth's crammed with heaven, and every common bush afire with God." These statements poetically echo truths conveyed many times in Scripture. The Talmud of early Jewish rabbinical writings boldly asserts, "God fills the universe."

SUMMARY

General morality universally applied springs from the reality that man is made in the image of God, and in fact is a little lower than the angels (Psa. 8:5). God designed man to respond to this general revelation, and to learn the particulars of Natural Law through experience and education. As this law is written in hearts, it becomes the rule by which men will account to God, as it has been from the beginning of time, and so shall ever be as long as the world continues. Established on this general revelation is the great saving principle of grace through faith in Christ and reliance upon Jesus as the source of righteousness and sanctification (I Cor. 1:30, II Tim. 1:8-10, Titus 3:4-7).

Even in the absence of special prophet- and apostle-given written instruction, every society nevertheless realizes that certain things are right and other things are wrong, and people can discern among various degrees of good or evil because Natural Law. Neither the people formally in covenant nor those outside of it always live up to the divine standard. And so, God had to make allowances for man's sins and hard heartedness (Matt. 19:8, Mark 10:5), through his constant love, mercy and forgiveness.

Every man to some degree wishes to seek after God (Eccl. 7:29) "who made man upright," straightforward. God has also set in the heart of man an intense awareness in the heart of more than the temporal. Man is not inherently righteous, but he does have a natural capacity for seeking the good. As his trained conscience recognizes what is right, he can look for God and find Him (Acts 17:27). Not just the intelligent but also those with "honest and good hearts" will bear fruit with patience. The difference between people, therefore, is not in possessing an ability to read or understand biblical teaching, but in whether a man allows his mind to be encumbered by myths, biases, tyrannies, or judgmental, legalistic attitudes, or any other irrationality which might hinder and even negate responsible thought and action.

CHAPTER FOUR

◇◇◇◇◇◇◇◇◇◇◇◇◇◇

THE CONSCIENCE: UNDENIABLE PROOF OF A MORAL REALM

As part of the creation, the conscience is a divine gift from God instilled in the minds of all people, endowing them with the capacity to make moral decisions. It is an innate awareness that one should be honest with self about right and wrong behavior. A properly trained conscience's great restraining or constraining power either accuses or excuses all actions and motives, pronouncing judgment upon propriety, commending the good and condemning the bad (see Rom. 2:14-15).

The Latin words which are translated conscience, *cum scio*, mean "with knowledge" or knowledge shared with. The individual's inner sense of right and wrong pronounces judgment upon himself, on both thoughts and actions. Coupled with an inner general framework of moral awareness, the conscience has a positive protective purpose as it constantly regulates reasoned human behavior, various specific rights and wrongs which have been learned through education and life's experiences. Without this inner witness, man would merely be a high animal form. Indeed, there is a profound difference between "I ought" and "I itch." Otherwise, neither term has anything to do with morality and all actions are physically caused.

Henry C. Sheldon has stated succinctly: "Conscience, if the term be taken in its broader meaning, is inclusive of three different elements: a perception of moral distinctions, a sense of obligations to the right, as opposed to the wrong, and a feeling of self-approbation or self-condemnation according as the act corresponds to the judgment of right and wrong. The first is undoubtedly subject to limitations.

"A man is not born an infallible moralist any more than he is born an infallible mathematician. But as he is implicitly a mathematician at birth, being endowed with a mental constitution which is intrinsically suited to recognize the relations of numbers, so he is implicitly a moralist at birth, being possessed of a moral constitution suited to recognize moral relations."

Early Christian writers referred to the functions of conscience and the reality of moral law. Late in the second century, Irenaeus, in *Against Heresies* (IV.15.1-2) wrote, "They [the Jews] had therefore a law, a course of discipline, and a prophecy of future things. God at the first, indeed [warned] them by means of natural precepts, which from the beginning He had implanted in mankind...." These moral laws upon the heart, he added, had to be embodied in the Ten Commandments, because Jews had abused their liberty and because of the hardness of their hearts.

The prolific early third century commentator Origen of Egypt, in His *De Principiis Significantus*, devotes Chapter Five, Section Two to the subject of our rational natures. He states the great universal truth that "every being...is endowed with reason, [and when transgressing] its statutes and limitations, is undoubtedly involved in sin, by swerving from rectitude and justice. Every rational creature, therefore, is capable of earning praise and censure: of praise, if in conformity to that reason which he possesses, he advances to better things; of censure, if he falls away from the plan and course of rectitude, for which reason he is justly liable to pains and penalties."

In contemplating moral distinctions, man does not know automatically the specifics of the rightness and wrongness of various acts, but the conscience points to an awareness of a moral realm where there is right and wrong. Though people might distinguish between these from different perspectives, everyone agrees that distinctions are to be made. Man is obligated to do the good and not the evil. Even when bad things are done, the perpetrator demonstrates the existence of conscience by justifying in some way the act in order to attain a desired goal, attributing the deed to a good motive.

Thus, everyone has a God-instilled, indestructible conscience which, when coupled with reason, sets before everyone two distinct moral paths—a general right way and a wrong way (see Chapter Ten). These great restraining and constraining forces lead to rigorous searching and testing of conduct. Conscience is easily abused or channeled negatively by various irrational acts and thoughts, including prejudice, ignorance, willful disregard of moral law, closed mindedness, and the like. When violated, the conscience may ultimately be defiled or even seared as with a hot iron, but it is fully destroyed only at death.

Romans 2:14-15, 25-29 inextricably ties conscience to the "law in the heart." Though the children of Israel had the Law of Moses, right-thinking Gentiles had obedience to conscience as a prerequisite to maintaining a right heart. Submission to inner light indisputably implies the existence of a higher Being who excused them in their well-doing, while violation of conscience "accused" them because of evil deeds (see Chapter Five).

In ancient times excused Gentiles had the quality of faith that accounted them as righteous, thus free from sin. God declared such people righteous. In his day Paul told the Romans that these doers of good had "honor and glory and peace" (2:6). Because of the moral law in the heart, a concept of a Higher Power who directed through conscience, there was incentive to the Gentile for right conduct. All who positively looked to the Creator knew idolatry was irrational, and thus sinful. These Gentiles knew that duty existed, and that good and evil could be discerned because of an inner sense of ought in their consciences which guided them to the specifics of moral law.

Faithfulness to this innate awareness of good and evil brought acceptance to the Gentiles. Just as in covenant Israel there were numerous wicked people, many Gentiles were sinners against conscience. But also among each of these were faithful people who lived up to their understanding of right and wrong. Even today, neither non-covenant people nor Christians gain salvation before God through adherence to a structured law system, a legal code. All believers are equal before God. What might save the Christian might save the Gentile; what condemns one condemns the other.

As aptly stated by R. L. Kilpatrick, the law written on the heart is, within the framework of understanding, "nothing more than having the will of God in the conscience, formed by way of knowledge. Rather than conscience being an unsafe guide, it is the only guide, and not only that it is an infallible guide. The conscience is that which renders infallible judgments and decisions. To say that the conscience is infallible is not to say that it is *divinely* infallible."

Conscience thus backs up moral judgment. A pleasurable feeling comes by doing what right; the pain of a guilty conscience results when thinking and doing wrong. When a person sincerely accepts the guilt emanating from his conscience, thereby recognizing that he has sinned and stands in need of God's grace and forgiveness, the stage is set for further encounters with God's will disclosed in nature and in the moral law and (if available) the special revelation of Scripture.

And so, because man is created in God's image (Gen. 1:27, 9:6), he has God's moral law in his heart, written in his mind through reason which reflects upon good and evil, recognition and revelation, all acquired during the course of life's ongoing experiences. Man's conscience bears witness to these universal truths however acquired, and renders judicial decisions as to whether they are being followed, punishing or approving various actions.

TRAINING THE CONSCIENCE

Throughout time, God has embedded in the conscience of every man a general moral awareness. This built-in faculty monitors all behavior, and when it is healthy, it pushes every person toward a desire to choose right actions and avoid wrong ones. At birth, this inner sense of ought is like the broad frame of an artist's blank canvas. The picture within acquires the specifics of good and evil and other definition during a lifetime of maturation, education, and in the reasoning out of life's situations and in the interpretation of everyday ethical choices. These things point to the reality of *general* revelation, and are experienced by all people throughout time.

The *special* revelation as recorded in the Bible did not initiate moral law; long before the introduction of Scripture various actions by one person toward another were *already* helpful and right and enhanced relationships, or they were destructive and wrong in that they diminished the rights of others and the principle of equality, the heritage of an impartial God. Almost every viable society recognizes these things, even if it does not acknowledge the Source.

In a real sense, our conscience *is* us. As perceptions change and various ethical choices made, the conscience matures, fleshes out. The ethical makeup of all people is therefore necessarily different. Though Christians share various gospel fundamentals, including a belief in the existence of the one spirit Creator-God and the authority of His son, vast differences often exist in the details of various beliefs, because of education and environmental influences and those among fellow believers. Since God's children do not believe alike about the teachings of *special* revelation, it should be evident that non-covenanters do not precisely hold alike what might be learned from observation and reason—morals and ethics of *general* revelation (Rom. 1:20).

The God-endowed general course of a right way and a wrong way is solidly based upon His nature. Through reason and acquired knowledge, the moral law written on the mind and the conscience judges all actions according to that heavenly standard. The more knowledge added to a God fearer's basic desire to do right, the closer he comes to essential truth. It is precisely in this way that the conscience becomes enlightened. Even if the light is barely visible, everyone recognizes the direction toward the light, for Jesus the ultimate light declared, "He that does the truth cometh to the light" (John 3:21a).

In the course of learning about specifically what is right and wrong, the conscience can be trained in the way of righteousness. But it also can harbor misinformation and incomplete moral judgment. By elimination of superstition and other irrationalities which perpetuate ignorance, anyone can usually arrive at the principles of natural morality through reason, education and experience.

Though Saul of Tarsus had been living up to a good conscience (Acts 23:1), he erred by thinking that God was pleased when he persecuted people of the Way (Acts 7:59). Throughout his life Saul followed his conscience in its current understanding. Instead of an unsafe conscience, Saul's knowledge was faulty and misguided, for he did not understand that imprisoning disciples of Christ and breathing threats against them was clearly contrary to God's will (Acts 9:1, 26:9).

In contrast, a live, tender conscience executes right moral judgment as much as possible in all matters. Everyone's conscience is responsible for its acquired truth; as new ones are understood, the ever-dynamic conscience changes. This is precisely what the righteous Gentile Cornelius did after hearing about Christ (Acts 10-11). An increase in knowledge brought to him an obligation to act upon the additional light shed upon him. By never willfully rejecting moral truths everyone can strive to form correct judgments and execute them righteously and fairly, constantly giving heed to the urging of a good conscience.

Hellenistic statue of ancient orator, as was the apostle Paul (Acts 17:22).

CHAPTER FIVE
◇◇◇◇◇◇◇◇◇◇◇◇

A COVENANT IN PRINCIPLE: THE LAW IN THE HEART

Chapters One, Two and Three introduce the concept of the universally applied and generally revealed Natural Law, evidence of which is also found throughout both the Old and New Testaments. This disclosure is revealed in the creation and an inner sense of ought (Rom.1:19-20), something embedded in everyone's conscience, as explained in Chapter Four.

In Romans 2:6-15, the apostle Paul defines this general revelation as the "law written in the heart" (v. 14), on every man (vv. 6, 9) in view of God's final judgment (vv. 7-8). This includes Jews and also Gentiles are further identified as the circumcised and the uncircumcised respectively (vv. 2:26-29). Natural Law is the measure for judgment at the end-time for everyone, whether living before or after the cross of Christ. Additionally, anyone in a formal covenant with God is also subject to prophetic and apostolic special revelation, to the extent that it is understood, as explained in Chapter Seven.

As righteous Gentiles in any era find God's approval, they are "excused" in the sight of heaven (v. 15) and the blood of Christ washes away their sins. However, tradition insists that since the day of Pentecost of Acts 2, God somehow changed the standard of present acceptance of good people which never have been exposed to gospel teaching. While admitting that God-fearing Gentiles outside of the formal covenant in Old Testament times did secure a positive standing, now right-hearted people this side of the cross possess no glorious hope of salvation because it is available only to those who have heard and obeyed the gospel of Christ. This arbitrary pronouncement is rendered despite the good character of these many non-covenanters and their respect and service of the true spirit God of heaven.

Even if those pious ones who possess godly fear yet live outside of the family of Christ should not currently possess salvation with God, this does not mean that they lack some measure of positive consideration in heaven, because of their good intent, heart-obedience and right living. God indeed provides them a defense, "their conscience bearing witness" (Rom. 2:15), because through their innate sense they positively behave as the law demands, though lacking the written guidance of Scripture. The doctrine of salvation is less about a final destiny—heaven—as it is statement about a current positive relationship with God of people properly responding to known truth, year in, year out (see Chapter Nine).

Stated another way, while these right-doing people outside of a formal covenant with God may not be assured of ultimate salvation, it is far more improper to consider them as hell bound. These determinations are made strictly by the Judge; no one should "whittle on God's end of the stick" by rendering negative judgment upon moral people with excused consciences. Any Christian exceeds his place by making decisions about a righteous one's present acceptance, for Christ himself condemned these kinds of judicial pronouncements (Matt. 7:1-5).

THE LAW IN THE HEART

When Gentiles do by nature what is right in keeping with moral law, a covenant in principle has been established between them and God. Though never hearing the gospel of Christ (much less obeying it) and thus not formally in covenant with God, they live life the best they can with knowledge of heavenly things in their current understanding of God's will, their available light.

Throughout the entire of Romans 2, Paul established a case for a secure position for these right-living ones who are seemingly like confident passengers on a small vessel at sea. They are not lost as they steer their ship on course by the generally revealed moral truths of Natural Law. Their helm is fixed on respecting the Creator and living according to conscience, ever seeking greater light, doing good and shunning evil.

If the ship of Christ should sail alongside, these good hearts would cross over after introduction to the greater light and thus maintain their position out of the water. In entering a formal peace covenant with God, they would thereafter enjoy the fullness of heavenly blessings and favors possessed by anyone else who has similarly entered into a relationship with Christ.

Though Paul does not introduce the phrase "law in the heart" until verse 14, important aspects of moral awareness appear as early as verse 5. In absolute righteousness, God will judge every man by this code "according to his deeds..." (vv. 5, 10). "Glory and honor and immortality, eternal life" (vv. 6-7a) will be granted to those who "persevere in doing good" (v. 7b), while the wrath and indignation of

1:18 will be meted to the unrighteous, who do not align their lives with moral truth (v. 8). Everyone throughout time will be judged by this positive universal standard of right living.

The ones doing good deeds and living morally, Jews and Gentiles alike (v. 10), are presently accepted and will be accorded "glory and honor and peace," while all evildoers will experience distress and tribulation (v. 9). God never exhibits favoritism in respect to those failing to do good or practice evil (v. 11). Sinners under general law will perish (v. 12), since only the doers of the law will be justified, accounted as righteous (v. 13).

The word "for" in verse 14 invites a conclusion, and climaxes Paul's reasoning which had unfolded in the preceding eight verses, expressly developing the Natural Law concept: "For when Gentiles not having the law do through their innate sense the [moral] things of the law, these are a law to themselves, in that they demonstrate the effect of the law written in their hearts, their consciences bearing witness, and their thoughts alternately accusing or defending them" (vv. 14-15).

These verses plainly show that righteous people not in a formal covenant with God, and thus not subject to special biblical revelation, nevertheless through their behavior clearly demonstrate that they possess moral truths which they live by through Natural Law. They behave as the law commands in the absence of written instruction. These good hearts are fully aware of the Creator and an inner sense of ought (Rom. 1:19). Their consciences pass judgment in their lives, either "accusing" or "excusing" them by defending their thoughts, attitudes, words, and outward deeds or inner secrets, whether past, present, or contemplated. They possess a definite moral standard, a "law unto themselves," and their present acceptance (salvation) before God is based on faithfulness to it.

These righteous, discerning people have developed their lives in harmony with their sense of available light. But if all present day God-believing non-covenanters are hell-bound, as tradition insists, why would it matter whether or not their consciences "accuse" or "excuse" them (Rom. 2:14-15)? Evidently, these righteous ones are judged solely by Natural Law, not by a covenantal standard which involves hearing and submitting to the gospel of Christ and other New Testament instruction.

Right-living doers of good possess a sense of discernment etched upon their hearts. Sin is not engraved upon their thoughts and minds (Jer. 17:1). The metaphorical expression "written on the heart" signifies not only that non-covenanters know certain things to be right, but also feel compelled by conscience to do them. However, they "cease to be a law to themselves the moment their knowledge becomes vicious and leads them to do wrong" (Moses Lard, *Commentary on Romans*, p. 87-88). How very plain is this teaching.

As with Christians, God will judge non-covenanters with a view toward granting them eternal life or destruction, by looking into their hearts to see if they have lived consistently with the dictates of their own conscience, namely, how well they have adhered to the measure of moral truth they have attained. Their standing before God is further determined by how they judge others, day-in and day-out. They stand self-condemned if they do not abide by their own standard if they accuse others for acts they practice themselves (Rom. 2:1-2). On the other hand, those applying moral principles impartially to self and neighbor, are spared the wrath of God.

Righteous people "patiently doing good" receive every consideration from God whatever their time and circumstance (vv. 7, 10). Such ones avoiding evil (v. 9) are in general accord with God's will and moral principles; assuredly they *know* their Creator. They are "of a good constitution or nature" (Thayer); in their consistent eschewing of evil, they will not experience God's fury, the fate of evil persons filled with selfish ambition and bent on dishonoring God (v. 8). Everybody generally knows right from wrong in his heart.

The fundamental universal principles of Romans 2:6-15 reach a climax in verses 25-29, wherein Gentiles adhering to moral law are all given the status of "circumcised people"—i.e., precisely equivalent to being Christians, children of the covenant. This inner sense of right, coupled with a disposition to do well, is therefore more fundamental than various covenantal duties. As expressly taught in Romans 2:26, an uncircumcised Gentile habitually practicing the righteous requirements of law, will have his uncircumcision regarded as circumcision—a sign of a relationship and a pact with heaven, enjoying peace with God.

The non-covenanter who obeys moral precepts thus enjoys rights and honors specifically accorded Christians who have the benefit of special apostolic revelation and promises. In fact, these "outsiders" are far better off than covenant-sealed people who consistently fail to do His will. He will punish the disobedient who possess His special written laws but do not follow them, but instead engage in sin.

Paul declared that the real "Jew" refers to all people among the uncircumcision whose hearts are right before God (Rom. 2:29). The righteous circumcised in heart give the name "Jew" its rightful dignity and content, and are God's covenant children in principle. As A. T. Robertson aptly states, "This inward or inside Jew, who lives up to his covenant relation to God, is the high standard that Paul put before the merely professional Jew" (see Rom. 2:25).

Nevertheless, both Gentiles not in formal covenant and disciples of Christ stand condemned if their hearts do not adhere to the truths they comprehend (see Chapter Seven). Their "circumcision" then becomes "uncircumcision" (Rom. 2:26). But all persons with changed hearts and minds following the principles of moral living with noble intent partake of the Creator's blessings and enjoy His favor.

Being accepted of God never meant meticulous obedience to externals, the rote keeping of the letter of the law; it involves seeking truth and cultivating a God-consciousness by the inward man, the soul-life. Habitually doing good and overcoming evil is a matter of heart and spirit. Praise and commendation for these righteous ones are also from God, not from man (Rom. 2:29b). The non-covenanter's faith may be incomplete, imperfect, perhaps even rudimentary, but his positive acts are counted as if they were deeds flowing from a covenant relationship (v. 26).

And so, not merely a negative function in Romans 1:18-2:29, natural moral law upholds an acceptable relationship with the Creator. Indeed, God is not a respecter of persons (Gal. 2:16); He honors good character throughout the ages, and always comforts the right-hearted who are in league with Him and doing the right, the virtuous. God blesses them because in purpose and intent their heart circumcision means the dismissal of evil thoughts and deeds from their minds. Their "uncircumcision" is as "circumcision" (v. 29), a sign of a positive covenant relationship with God (Gen. 17:13-14, Acts 7:8).

In stark contrast to plain truth, tradition declares that these righteous ones have no chance of future glory, but instead are not God-accepted and thus are destined for judgment, because they never responded to the gospel of Christ (see Chapter Thirteen, Sections 1-3). Such teaching denies any credit to pious, heart-circumcised Gentiles who lead holy lives in righteousness. Thankfully, man is not the judge.

Throughout Romans 2 every good heart has experienced regeneration, renewal and acceptability before the Father. In "doing good" (vv. 7-10), and "showing the work of law" (v. 14), they serve God in newness of life (not by the letter of the law), walking in the spirit, just as right-thinking Christians do (Rom. 7:6; II Cor. 3:6; Gal. 5:16-23). Conversely, every evil person uncircumcised in heart faces judgment and destruction (Lev. 26:41; Deut. 10:16; Jer. 4:4, 9:26; Ezek. 44:7, Acts 7:51).

Therefore, right-thinking non-Christians unaware of gospel teaching nevertheless display the *law of love* in their hearts, and their thoughts and actions display *deeds of love*. Some who never heard of gospel preaching and the special revelation of Scripture will nevertheless find a suitable defense as they stand face to face in judgment before a merciful God, in that they perceived His will from truth they possessed, walking in their available light, responding wholeheartedly according to their ability and opportunity. This principle holds true from Old Testament times into the Christian era as well.

NATURE

The apostle Paul wrote that moral Gentiles do the things of the law "by nature" (Rom. 2:14-15)—that is, "without prompting or guidance coming from any written code, therefore, in a sense, spontaneously..." (Hendrickson, p. 97). "By nature" points to "forces born in us" (Beer) or "innate moral instinct" (Godet). For instance, it is natural to be kind to wife and children, neighbors, and even to strangers. It is natural to consider the poor and the helpless, to defend life, and to oppose criminal acts. It is unnatural to be pretentious or dishonest, or to practice deceit, backbiting, or haughtiness, thus allying oneself with evildoers (Rom. 1:29-31).

The word nature (*phusis*) means "natural sense, native conviction or knowledge, as opposed to what is learned by instruction and accompanied by training or proscribed by law...guided by their natural sense of what is right and proper" (Thayer, p. 660). "This sense of right is a representation of God's image. It is a beam of His own holiness, which cannot be altered or abolished anymore than the nature of good and evil can be changed" (Samuel Bolton, *The True Bond of Christian Freedom*, p. 59).

Conversely, doing wrong conflicts with man's innate nature and God's moral order. Certain evil acts are self-evident, just as the "works of the flesh" catalogued in Galatians 5:19-21 are plainly contrary to moral principles and the natural order of things. Gentiles not in formal covenant are familiar with drunkenness, anger, jealousy, and immorality, fully realizing that all who practice such things are to be rebuked, as at Corinth. Not only Christians but also Gentiles of educated conscience possess this knowledge "in them" (Rom. 1:19). Man's acquaintance with morality and proper response to it transcends time and place and all traditional biblical dispensations—Patriarchal, Mosaic, and Christian.

An extensive chapter in James Bales' *The Law in the Heart* solidly documents Greek, Roman, and other ancient writings which criticize specific types of sinful behavior worthy of punishment. The ancients also recognized virtuous behavior similar to Paul's "fruit of the spirit" (Gal: 5:22-23). Bible preaching is not necessary to demonstrate to the Gentiles the rightness or wrongness of various deeds. They stand on their own, are self-evident. The purpose of Bible teaching is to instruct these truth-seeking people in the way of the Lord more perfectly, introducing them to Jesus via the gospel.

The ethical make-up of various contemporary unchristianized nations and tribes may be quite developed even in the most primitive societies, despite the absence of the written biblical revelation. Long before any European intrusion in central Africa, certain Efe tribes of the Ituri Forest in Zaire honored the Creator by forbidding adultery, lying, theft, blasphemy, demon worship, and many other forms of misbehavior. They did not practice anti-moral cannibalism, body mutilation, sorcery, murder rituals, and cruelty to others. There is no proof of a connection between the unwritten law that Efe pygmies subject themselves to and any of God's revelations which various Christian missionaries later brought to them through Scripture. Their sense of morality appeared to be self-evident; God gave it to them and to thousands of other peoples and tribes.

Nigeria's Yoruba tribe has worshiped Olodumare, who to them is an all-powerful Creator they deem worthy of service and adoration by all of mankind. He is approachable as the Father and could not be represented by images. This One is the same God who is the Most High, and the King who dwells in the heavens, where He executes judgment (Psa. 75:7), discerning hearts by seeing both the inside and outside of every man (Heb. 4:12-13). Only the true God can accomplish creative work by speaking worlds into existence (Gen. 1:1-31, Heb. 11:5, Isa. 40:28).

Anthropological research has shown that belief in the Spirit God of Yoruba and Efe did not come about through contact with Christians. These tribesmen recognized their need to cast themselves upon a merciful personal God. Other isolated worshipers of the one God possess an amazing awareness of His nature and interaction with man through general revelation. Peru's Shapiro Indians recognize that they must be "strong on God" and be dependent on this spiritual Higher Power, and not to rely on personal strengths.

Many ancient Chinese and Koreans worshiped the one true God, as did some among the Incas in Peru, Ethiopians and various African tribes, and the Karen tribesmen in the jungles of Burma. In *Eternity in Their Hearts*, Don Richardson documents about 25 such cultures which worshiped not pagan gods but Yahweh, showing that the concept of a supreme God has existed for centuries in thousands of cultures worldwide.

Even certain North American Indians understand the deepest of spiritual concepts. In making peace with early American colonialists, various tribes recognized the importance of living soberly and kindly with their white brothers. Most knew that there is one Great Spirit whose power made the world and all things therein, and to whom all people owe their well being. They believed that every person must give an account for what he does in the world, for God has written His law on our hearts, by which they must recognize an obligation to love and help one another (and not to harm or engage in mischief).

Indeed, to one and all God has not left Himself without witness (Acts 14:16-17), setting a sense of eternity in the hearts of men in the absence of writings. Even more than general revelation, God somehow at various times had directly communicated various truths to these scattered peoples, as He did with Abraham, Melchizedek, Jethro, and many others well before the formal special revelation to the Old Testament prophets. The self-evident behavioral truths mentioned above are the core of Natural Law.

The list by C. S. Lewis of morality to be found in various cultures throughout time show a concurrence upon several specific laws, differing of course in application. These are (1) general beneficence; (2) special beneficence; (3) duties to elders; (4) duties to children; (5) law of justice; (6) good faith and veracity; (7) mercy; and (8) magnanimity (*Abolition of Man*, pp. 15-16).

In *Mere Christianity*, Lewis clearly delineates the moral law and conscience by relating a situation where a man hears a cry for help from another. He faces two desires, either to render aid or to keep out of danger. In addition to these two impulses "you will find inside you...a third thing which tells you that you ought to help and suppress the impulse to run away" (p. 8).

That which judges between the two desires deciding which impulse should be encouraged cannot itself be either of them. Lewis adds: "You might as well say that the sheet of music which tells you, at a given moment, to play one note on the piano, and not another, is itself one of the notes on the keyboard. The Moral Law tells you the tune we have to play; our instincts are merely the keys" (*ibid.*).

In addition to religious thinkers, even hard core Communist writers, hardly Christian, acknowledge as virtuous the Golden Rule, justice, truthfulness, integrity, moral and sexual cleanliness, honest labor, unselfishness, and gratitude. Communist bosses themselves have spoken out against murder, stealing, drunkenness, and other immoral acts. (Bales, *Communism and the Moral Law*, p. 156-158). They routinely make corrupt applications, yet the nature of reality forces these leaders to acknowledge a realm of conscience where there are choices and universal virtues.

Bales found among the Chinese, the Hindus, Greeks, Jews, Moslems, animists—in fact among virtually all people of all ages and races—an awareness of morality, for it is transcendent, originating with the Creator. "There is a law, above lawmaking and human lawmakers, to which the lawmakers themselves are subject....This power is power...whose workings man cannot ultimately frustrate...." (Bales, p. 156).

The distinctive expression "every tribe, tongue, people and nation..." (with slight variations) occurs seven times in the book of Revelation. Individuals embodied in that phrase coincide with worldwide prophesying (10:11), the preaching of the eternal gospel (14:6), the rule of the Roman Empire as depicted in the sea beast (13:7), the waters of society upon which the harlot Babylon sat (17:15; see also v. 1), and the extent of the great world city (11:8-9) mystically called "Sodom and Egypt."

Most significant of all, Revelation 5:9 and 7:9 plainly show that there will be blood-bought individuals from "every tribe, tongue, people and nation" before God's throne in heaven. Evidently, the multitude present in glory before God's throne will consist of far more than covenant Jews under Moses or the people of

Christ in this era. How? In addition to proclaiming God's written revelation, He has communicated with one and all of the created, past and present, the truths of creation and morality. All people everywhere potentially have this "better hope" (Heb. 7:19; cp. Eph. 4:4).

The number of people who will ultimately be in heaven will indeed be great, in fact, as numerous as seashore pebbles or stars in the sky (Gen. 15:5). The inhabitants of the "new earth" (Rev. 21-22) will consist of a "great multitude which no one can count," covenanters in moral lock step with non-covenanters (Rev. 7:9; see also 5:9, 13). Glory to God! Yet tradition insists that only a few will be saved. Through the principle of by whom and to whom, Jesus applied the "few" of the "straight and narrow way" (Matt. 7:13-14) to evil contemporaries (v. 11) and not across the face of mankind, past and present. For further response, see Chapter Thirteen, Section Six.

Even today, Bible-laden missionaries with the aid of modern communication will never reach several thousand of the world's separate people groups. Scripture still has not been translated into perhaps 2,500 tongues and dialects, and multiplied scores of other languages know of only a few New Testament books. Past natural calamities, wars and plagues have prevented evangelists from reaching untold numbers of peoples and nations, while some civilizations and small tribes have entirely disappeared without having heard preaching about Christ. Yet, some blood-bought righteous ones from each of these people groups will be represented among the countless multitude before the heavenly throne.

What God has written in the hearts of these people from every nation and tribe finds a response in each individual's conscience (see Chapter Four). The moral capacity and the rudimentary moral dimensions of conscience is God-given to everyone before birth. Then through education and experience it develops in a child as he moves forward into adulthood.

Though God has implanted a general moral awareness in the very mind of man (Rom.1:19), creation also has a great impact (v. 20). These are the extent of the Gentiles' available light, a standard for them to live and be judged by. Rejecting these universal realities is called "exchanging the truth of God for a lie" (Rom. 1:21, 25).

God's covenant people face similar condemnation if they do not accept New Testament truths to the extent that they understand them. People of faith, whether in or out of covenant with God, will be judged by their fidelity to whatever it was possible for them to know: to Gentiles the general moral law which is their high standard, and additionally to covenant ones Christ's teachings and principles. The Just One cannot and will not ask for more.

The Greek Stoics, in calling this moral law *phusus*, or nature, urged all men to live *kata phusin*, according to nature. Principles of health, as well as laws governing moral living, are broken at one's peril. Plutarch rhetorically asked, "Who shall govern the governor?" He answered, "Law, the king of all mortals and immortals ... which is not written on papyrus rolls or wooden tablets, but is his own reason within the soul, which perpetually dwells with him and guards him and never leaves his soul bereft of leadership."

Thus, in man's very nature is implanted a general awareness of ought; faithfulness to conscience brings a degree of acceptability. Apart from apostolic and prophetic revelation, righteous people throughout the world know that (1) the Creator-God exists; (2) all forms of idolatry are wrong; (3) good and evil are recognizable realities; (4) man is obligated to do the good; and (5) transgression of moral principles brings sin and guilt. It is all written in the heart.

Therefore, the "by nature" of Romans 2:14 means that: (1) Man has moral law in the heart or consciousness because of what he does; (2) man acts because of what this innate law teaches; and (3) this doing is not because of extraneous apostle- or prophet-revealed instruction, culture or influence beyond the endowments of nature (see Meyer, *New Testament Commentary*, p. 118).

MORAL LAW

Violation of moral law is specifically called sin in Romans 2:12. There is nothing vague about it. It is definite transgression as man's conscience convicts him of bad deeds. Therefore, the unwritten moral law in the heart is similar to mathematical and physical laws or any other law of nature which governs the universe and the development of every living thing. All of these express God's power. Laws of straight thinking (logic) and health are similarly unwritten.

The innate moral law is made evident in man's capacity to behave in either right or wrong ways as he interacts in society. It did not originate nor pass away with God's establishment of formal covenantal revelations to holy men of old. Moral principles guide everyone who has entered God's eternal peace pact, first with the Patriarchs and then with Jews and later with the people of Christ, but these very principles also serve those outside of a formal covenant, as Romans 2:6-29 distinctly teaches.

From the time of Adam forward, people have lived responsibly to their present truth of creation and morals, apart from special biblical revelation, oral or written. Abraham and his kinsman, including Lot, Melchizedek, and the righteous people associated with them, though all justified by God, could still sin against God's moral law, as did the Amorites (Gen. 15:16). Sodom and Gomorrah were under this law (Gen 4:2, 10); some of these people were wicked (Gen. 18:20-22), yet righteous others (v. 23) were ultimately physically spared (vv. 3-33) and will yet be spiritually delivered (Matt. 10:15).

These people were either grievous sinners or accounted as acceptable before God in the days of the Patriarchs and afterwards. There were also untold numbers of righteous people during the centuries when the Law of Moses guided the nation. Various "excused" non-covenant people lived throughout the Roman Empire at the time of the Pentecost of Acts 2, and for decades afterwards, and they exist today, and all subject to Natural Law. When they sin they fall short of this God-given unwritten moral standard. A commitment to the truths of creation and moral precepts determine if they are virtuous or wicked. No guilt can be associated with these people for not obeying Christ's gospel, for they have never come in contact with it.

Therefore, the righteous ones of Romans 2:6-15 consist of a long line of individuals throughout time from every country and people group. Revelation 5:9, 13 shows that these blood-bought individuals arise from every tongue, tribe, and nation. They comprise a great multitude which no one can count (7:9), and each are clothed in victory robes and waving palm branches.

Though not subject to instruction which regulate the people of Christ, these non-covenanters are nevertheless accepted of God, saved, based on their behavior in responding to the law in the heart. Any similarities between law which guides Christians and the Gentiles' law engraven upon the heart no more shows that the latter are subject to a legalistically contrived "covenant law," than it proves that the Gentiles were under the law of Moses (Bales, *The Law in the Heart*, p. 160).

General moral law, written and embedded in man's nature, furnishes vital truths concerning the one true spirit Creator. For everyone there is a responsibility to walk in them (see Phil. 3:16). However, moral law was not meant to be sufficient, for God through prophets and apostles further revealed to covenant ones His special will in statements, commandments, and Scripture illustrations which further elaborate upon moral precepts. Neither body of truth may be rejected or suppressed without incurring God's displeasure. Additionally, in Old Testament times the prophets set forth ceremonial laws which, though not of a moral nature, nevertheless needed to be followed by Israel.

THE LAW IN THE HEART TODAY

Does God presently judge all of His creation solely on the basis of special revelation, the Bible? Evidently not. Moral goodness exalts the non-covenant person now, just as it did for him before the cross. Unrighteousness brings forth God's wrath and judgment upon all people in any era. No better evidence is needed to prove the constancy of unwritten moral law than the existence of gravity, a survival instinct, love of offspring, self-preservation and various other unchangeable non-physical realities.

Two fundamental principles underlie all religious/moral righteousness: total love of God and love of neighbor as self. These are the essence of all specific moral precepts. Simply stated, God's law centers upon the Golden Rule (Mark 12:29-31). These have been in continuous existence since Genesis.

All men have a basic sense of ought and duty, though they may perceive the details of morality in diverse ways. Though earthly societies obviously differ on how many wives a man can have, none believe that a man may simply take anyone else's wife at his pleasure. Even the most evil people have some sense of right and wrong, perhaps dim and elementary but nevertheless present, for God has set it there in the conscience.

A moral sense is therefore etched upon the minds of all people. Throughout time the creation continually shouts, "Our God, He is alive!" When anyone refuses to allow this *gnosis* (knowledge of God) to become *epignosis* (realization or mental comprehension), and thereby fails to allow moral teachings to actively transform his life, God's wrath will continually pour forth upon him. II Tim 3:2-9 shows that people without natural affection, the heartless, the intractable, and the like, will not be glorified by resurrection at the time when Jesus will return.

Romans 2:6-14 discloses that the modern non-covenanter will be judged for better of worse by the law of conscience and the continual revelation of the creation. "For as many as have sinned with the law…" (v. 12) is stated in the "constant timeless aorist, covering all time" (Shepard, *Life and Letters of Paul*, p. 372). Since Paul set forth both sin and the law in the heart as continuous (Rom. 2:15, Heb. 8:10), the possibility remains that conscientious Gentiles, even today and regardless of place, might be judged as righteous. If not, why not?

The presence of sin, the law in the heart, and continuous general revelation and all other elements in Romans 1:18-2:29 are expressed in the present tense, hence each is a modern *current* reality. Everyone is subject to this uninterrupted unfolding of God. The moral non-covenanter who reverences the Creator has an "excused" conscience is accounted as righteous, free from sin because of the life of Jesus Christ.

No New Testament writer stated that the moral law in the heart had ceased or was "nailed to the cross," as the Law of Moses allegedly was. How are the moral principles in the heart abolished without denying the very God-made nature within man? In Romans 2:12-16, Paul applied the truths of universal moral law to all then living, three decades after the cross. It existed then. It exists now.

God will render to everyone, in or out of covenant, according to his deeds (Rom. 2:6-9), for in Him there is no respect of persons, treating each as he deserves, good or bad (v. 11). The Jewish prophets stated these principles (Job

34:11; Psalm 62:12; Prov. 24:12; Jer. 18:10, 32:19), and the apostles reaffirmed them (Matt. 16:27, Rom. 14:12, I Cor. 3:8, II Cor. 5:10; Rev. 2:23, 20:12, 22:12). Contemporary Gentiles stand before God based on their consistency of adherence to moral law as understood, not faithfulness to biblical truths and precepts which govern the covenantal family.

A time problem and a cruel paradox exists by insisting that conscientious non-covenant moral people who love God cannot be saved after the cross. If God judged these same Gentiles (who were not Jewish proselytes) as righteous before Christ came, and He did, does it not constitute partiality on His part not to judge these people similarly today? Would not present-day moral God-fearers have been better off living before the cross? Why does that event arbitrarily separate Gentiles of Old Testament times from those living in the Christian era?

If the latter live under an alleged "new law" for their judgment, does not such a distinction directly contradict Peter's words in Acts 10:34-35, a verse which unmistakably declares that God does not show favoritism? The stated universal rule is plain: God is not one to show partiality, but throughout history morally right God-fearers are acceptable to Him.

No apostle ever suggested a change of status from the first century onward of non-covenant people who adhere to moral principles and do not suppress presently understood truth. When that standard is transgressed by people of any time and place, sin results. Those doing good and fearing the Creator are spared His wrath and destruction. As with the faithful of covenant, these God-devotees for all intents and purposes are dead to sin and circumcised in heart.

God is altogether just and righteous. He furnishes full protection to all who follow their conscientious understanding of truth, whether in or out of a formal covenant with Him. The Golden Rule and a proper recognition of duty toward God and fellow man, both flow from the holiness of God. The rewards He bestows, and the penalties He inflicts—all are righteous, for all men.

The faithful are pillars in God's temple (Rev. 3:12), while idolators lack this blessing.

CHAPTER SIX

CORNELIUS, SALVATION, AND THE GRACE OF GOD

The tale of the Roman centurion Cornelius as told in Acts 10-11 demonstrates God's unfathomable grace, brilliantly displayed in love and unselfish concern for a right-living, devoted follower of truth. Before embracing Christ, Cornelius as a believer in God was an "upright and God-fearing man" (10:22), reverent (v. 25) and obviously was not profane or unclean (v. 15). If accounted righteous, he was justified before God. If justified, then his sins were forgiven (Acts 10:43), thus saved.

God's continual acceptance of Cornelius was on the basis of his virtue, truth, good will, honesty, and absolute sincerity before God in the absence of ritual. He was a God-possessed refugee from the pagan world, a sheep not of the Jewish fold (John 10:16). He admired and followed the Jewish religion, stopping short of circumcision. In this state the one true Shepherd continually guarded him, cared for him. Cornelius was called to holiness, and lived day by day in an atmosphere of present acceptance and comfort.

The key to understanding the story about Cornelius is Acts 10:34-35, a scripture which exhibits a principle which goes right across the board of humanity throughout time. Here, Peter understood that "God is not one to show partiality, but in every nation the man who fears Him and does what is right is welcomed to Him." This statement shows Heaven's saving justice, and contradicts man-devised steps and contrived patterns of law concerning salvation.

Acts 10:2-3 records several positive characteristics of this God-seeking Gentile:

(1) *Devout.* Cornelius was in the same company as saved people like the righteous Simeon (Luke 2:25), about three thousands godly Jews in Jerusalem on the day of Pentecost (Acts 2:5), faithful ones who buried Stephen (Acts 8:2), Ananias (Acts 22:12), an untold number of righteous proselytes and Jews in Pisidian Antioch (Acts 13:16, 26), numerous Jewish worthies recorded in Hebrews 11:5-39, as well as God-fearing hearts in several cities of the Roman world during the time Paul worked in Gentile country (Acts 13-19). The lives of Cornelius and these godly individuals like him centered upon a commitment to God. Certainly none were children of the devil; God had not damned any of them. Those whom God has cleansed, let no man call common (see Acts 11:14)...or unsaved!

Though one Greek word for "devout" (*sebomai*) might refer to merely being devoted to a religion, as in Acts 13:50, 17:4 and 17 and thus may not address salvation, much more often devout is *eulabes*, which means "taking hold well...careful as to the realization of the presence and claims of God, reverencing God, pious" (Thayer) as in Acts 2:5, 10:2, 22:12 and elsewhere. (see also W. E. Vine, *Expository Dictionary of New Testament Words*, pp. 309-310). Every instance of *eulabes* and an associative word *eusebes* points to people in a positive, acceptable state before God, saved.

(2) *Feared God.* This is healthy reverence as possessed by Noah while he prepared the ark (Heb. 11:7). In Hebrews 12:28, godly fear is associated with acceptable service and an awe of God. Jesus was heard because of his piety and devotion to the Father. All of these things are embodied in "fearing God." Acts 10:22 describes Cornelius as a "righteous and a God-fearing man."

(3) *Gave Alms.* These are both deeds and gifts of charity to Jewish causes and involves being merciful. Alms deeds are associated with uprightness in Matthew 6:1. Mercy is directly related to covenant in Deuteronomy 7:7-9.

(4) *Prayed to God Continually.* In thus seeking God, Cornelius was a worshiper of the Creator of the universe who had placed all living things on earth. His requests had ascended as a memorial before heaven. Lydia similarly revered God; other women with whom she associated were devoted to prayer (Acts 16:13-14). Titius Justus was still another of God's servants (Acts 18:7).

(5) *A Truth Seeker.* In view of all of Acts 10-11, Cornelius was continually faithful to the degree of light which he possessed, and maintained a disposition to obey all the truth he could find, embracing additional truth (light) when exposed to it. Cornelius demonstrated this attitude by

SPEAKING SAVING WORDS 63

readily accepting Christ in response to Peter's preaching. In doing so, he gained the gift of the Holy Spirit and a formal covenant status with God.

Had he rejected Peter's additional instruction after understanding it, he would not be a seeker of truth, and thus would have jeopardized his acceptability before God. Instead, Cornelius readily embraced the light of Christ, culminating in baptism (Acts 10:48). Here is indeed a splendid example of believing through grace, for "those who believe in Him receive the remission of sins" (Acts 10:43). This process also is called "repentance that leads to life" (Acts 11:18).

Heaven does not show partiality, and God keeps as His own all righteous individuals who respect Him and do the morally right. Just as the life of Christ as the "holy one" was set apart from others (Acts 2:27, 13:35), so were the devout ones listed above. Cornelius' character centered on a commitment to God. As a seeker of righteousness and living a life of holiness, what more could God have required of Cornelius prior to hearing the preaching of Peter?

SPEAKING SAVING WORDS

Despite the extensive positive evidence of Cornelius' good standing before God, contemporary legalism sternly maintains that he was unsaved until after his formal baptism into Christ. Cited as a proof text is Acts 11:14, "and he shall speak words to you by which you will be saved...." This appears to be a case of not seeing the forest for the trees, inasmuch as Cornelius enjoyed far more than a rudimentary faith relationship with God.

All who might differ with this conclusion need to show why devout people like Cornelius are presently unsaved and condemned. In fact, no negative evidence about his character appears in Acts 10-11 to point to an unsatisfactory relationship with God before the day that he accepted Christ. Rather, Cornelius responded to the gospel spoken by Peter so that he might *continue* to enjoy a safe status with God, so that his faith would grow deeper and better (as per the theme of the epistle to Hebrews), and develop an even fuller realization of truth than what he possessed before he met Peter. Through it all, his walk in God's light on the path of holiness was uninterrupted.

Before the time of Acts 10, Cornelius enjoyed an informal covenant with his Creator because of Romans 2:6-14. This God-devotee's faithfulness to moral principles was reckoned as circumcision, covenant loyalty (vv. 25-29). At peace with God, he remained in Heaven's care and never was in spiritual peril. And so, when Cornelius heard Christ's gospel through Peter, he readily accepted additional truth and entered into a formal covenant with God, yet all the while continuing in His favor.

The centurion was precisely a man after God's own heart, mindful to obey Him and never turning from truth. Like the three thousand or so on Pentecost, Cornelius promptly responded to Christ's gospel (Acts 2:38, 10:47-48). His continual acceptance clearly shows that God is interested in redeeming and serving people, not in constantly judging people and declaring them lost. Jesus said, "For God did not send His son into the world in order to condemn it, but that the world might be saved through Him" (John 3:17). Instead, God looks for right behavior and good hearts, and abides and comforts everyone who diligently seeks Him. He is eminently fair and merciful, for "saving justice and fair judgment are the foundation of His throne" (Psa. 89:14, 97:2-3).

This is dramatically the opposite of legalism's impersonal, judgmental attitude which actually discourages strong, godly relationships in its condemnation of all who do not live up to its human legal standard of acceptance and approval. God's law of love transcends man's puny inordinate love of the law; His Christ reaches out and touches the world's Cornelius people, searching their thoughts and intent of their hearts (Heb. 4:12), guarding as his own with equity all who are doing right and willing to accept additional truth. As the Father of mercy, God is eminently fair, and he continually abides with seekers of truth and righteousness.

Considering Acts 11:14 further, one could say, " I am coming to Dallas. I want to impart certain Bible truths to you (or perhaps a spiritual gift, as in Romans 1:11). I'm going to speak to you 'words of truth by which you will be saved...'" Such a statement obviously does not preclude them from *already* possessing truths or spiritual gifts and even salvation. Who would foolishly conclude that the gospel had never been available in Rome before Paul's arrival? Messianic Jews after the day of the Pentecost of Acts 2 likely took it there a score of years earlier (see vv. 5-10).

In the Olivet discourse Jesus said to the disciples in Matthew 24:13, "He that endures to the end shall [will] be saved"—the very words which appear in Acts 11:14 concerning Cornelius. Just as the phrase "shall be saved" addressed to Jesus' disciples in Matthew 24 does not mean that they were *presently* lost, but rather were in a God-approved state, likewise when Cornelius heard the same words he was not then bereft of enjoying God's favor and safety. To remain in covenant and continue to receive God's blessings, the disciples whom Jesus addressed had to "endure to the end." Similarly, Cornelius had to accept additional instruction as taught by Peter in order to be assured of continuance of God's favor.

Consider the righteous patriarch Abraham, a man whom James plainly declared "justified by works" (Jas. 2:21), a reference to a situation described in Genesis 22. Yet many years earlier, in Genesis 12, he was justified (declared righteous) by faith. Scripture is mishandled if, on the basis of James 2, it is assumed that Abraham was not accounted righteous, saved until the later time. Also, Jesus said to Zaccheus,

"Salvation has come to this house," (Luke 19:9). As a son of Abraham and in covenant with God, he was *already* saved. Therefore, it is indefensible to conclude on the basis of Acts 11:14 that Cornelius could not have been God-approved until after he responded to Peter's preaching (Acts 10:44-48).

Therefore, Acts 11:14 is not so much a statement on how to become saved; instead it shows how salvation is universally provided for and is available to *all* people. The overriding question is, what did Peter gain from the vision that he received (Acts 10:11-16)? He learned that Cornelius feared God and worked righteousness. Essentially, God said to him, "Now, since you see that I am no respecter of persons, and such devout God-fearers as Cornelius are acceptable to me, go preach to him as I have commanded you to do." Is this not what Peter learned? Otherwise, there was no point to the vision and Peter did not learn anything.

And so, the statement of Acts 11:14 regarding salvation does not necessarily mean that Cornelius was unsaved. He should be left as Luke in Acts 10-11 portrayed him: a devout worshiper of the one Creator-God. Declaring Cornelius lost is surely a case of boxing God into stridency and does not respect Heaven's acknowledgment of what holiness and character are all about. Cornelius is ever described as presently accepted of God and in service to both Jewish people and his fellow Roman citizens.

JESUS' OTHER SHEEP IN CORINTH

Righteous people like Cornelius are among those whom Jesus may have had in mind when Jesus said, "I have [now have—present, not future possession] other sheep that are not of this [Jewish] fold. I must bring them also" (John 10:16). Gathering scattered people is a function of God (Ezek. 34:13, 36:24, Jer. 32:37, Deut. 30:3-4). Other among the sheep included various God-seeking people of faith in the Gentile community of Corinth, including Titius Justus, a "worshipper of God" (Acts 18:7).

Before Paul began to preach the gospel of Christ to the Corinthians, in about 50 A.D. on his second missionary journey, the Spirit said to him, "Do not fear... for I have [now have, *not* future possession] many people in this city" (Acts 18:10). The verb tense is the same usage as in John 10:16. Though various citizens of Corinth stood condemned because of immoral acts and idolatrous practices (I Cor. 6:9-10), God specially described "many" in the city as His people. These believers did not enjoy a formal covenant with God, and they were certainly not baptized believers, yet the text plainly states that God possessed them as a present possession, guided by Natural Law. Various Corinthians following their available light had gained favor with the Creator.

The limited truth that these God-fearers faithfully obeyed not only brought guilt of sin when they violated their conscience, but it also served as the foundation upon which to accept the gospel of Christ and gain covenant status with God. These good-hearted Corinthians of God's possession are the very ones who would accept the truth of Christ and respond to it in baptism.

And so, Paul carried the gospel to Corinth, for example, to bring about a greater harvest of souls, since careful cultivation produces a better crop. The author of the book of Hebrews claims that knowledge of Christ and his teaching is "better" in every way. Further, in his ministry Jesus amplified moral law to its brightest and fullest expression. Telling others about Christ would purify the souls of the many Corinthians whom God already possessed.

These right-thinking Gentiles accepted additional knowledge unto obedience as preached by Paul, or their right standing before God would be in jeopardy. Persistent rejection of the gospel, if it is understood, would show that their hearts were not right. But would these righteous Corinthians who were unexposed to the better teaching of Christ perish, as alleged? It is often asserted that God will damn all of them because they did not proceed through the steps of the "gospel plan of salvation," even though they never had opportunities to hear the truth about Christ and believe them.

This manner of judgment certainly implies a most unacceptable view of God, making Him appear hard and demanding, reflecting negatively upon His justice (Psa. 89:14, 97:2). The loving Father in heaven wishes to bring all people of faith and goodness home with Him, as shown in the parable of the Prodigal Son (Luke 15:11-35). The righteous Judge takes no pleasure in sentencing any segment of His creation to death (John 3:17).

Gospel fruit bearing did not stop with these many good Corinthian hearts. Even among evildoers there were people whose hearts had been pierced by Paul's preaching, and they forsook adultery, drunkenness and other types of sinful behavior (I Cor. 6:9-11). As they submitted to the gospel, God added them to the community of formally covenanted ones. Good deeds and loving attitudes also can resurrect a stunted belief and bring about an attitude to hear preaching about Christ and enter into a formal covenant union with the God of heaven.

These righteous Corinthians had a measure of faith, as did an untold number of upright non-covenant people with whom Paul came in contact during his first two missionary journeys. At Pisidian Antioch, Paul addressed "men of Israel and those who fear God"—Jews and Gentiles (Acts 13:16, 26, 43, 50). Lydia was a "worshiper of God," implying acceptability before she heard the gospel of Christ (Acts 16:14). In Thessalonica, a number of God-fearing Greeks embraced Christ and joined Paul and Silas (Acts 17:3-4); the same thing happened in Berea (v. 12).

Nothing is stated that these respecters of God strewn across the first century Roman Empire were subject to judgment. Instead, they honored and glorified the Creator while following known moral law and other truth about God to the best of their understanding. Some of these faith-filled Gentiles were Jewish proselytes who also followed Moses including circumcision, ceremonial offerings in the Jerusalem temple, and in the late Jewish period a form of baptism. Isaiah had prophesied about these good hearts (55:3-7) and thousands of pious Jews appeared in Jerusalem at Pentecost (Acts 2:5-10). They awaited apostolic preaching to learn about Jesus Christ, so that through the gospel they could perfect their understanding of the God of heaven and His ways.

Thus, in his day Jesus knew of many God-fearers among the nations who were not of the Jewish fold (John 10:16); these moral people of faith scattered abroad (11:52) now had to be called through the gospel. Nevertheless, a disposition to love which constantly moved these elected "sheep" to live godly lives was a sure sign that they were presently benefiting from Heaven's grace.

Instead of measuring up to a man-devised test to determine whether or not they were children of God, these "sheep" lived by the spirit of God which they expressed in loving, unselfish concern and helpfulness toward others, good faith, and in doing the morally right, shunning evil works. After all, this is precisely what a merciful Creator would expect. These righteous Gentiles yielded to their Shepherd's voice by following understood truth (see Chapter Seven).

In the shepherd analogy, it was not necessary that the sheep be identical, nor that they all follow in the same manner and believe the same things, nor did they need to be scrubbed clean before they were allowed to associate with the Herdsman; it was sufficient that they follow him. Note also that the father reunited in a similar way with his prodigal son caked with pig slop, asking no questions while welcoming him home (Luke 15:11-32).

All who recognize good and eschew evil are accepted of God based on the finished work of Jesus on the cross. Their positive responses may not always be expressions of a mature, explicit covenantal faith but merely a "mustard seed" measure of faith. Nevertheless, it is still the one faith of Ephesians 4:4, and potentially could be as strong as that possessed by a James or a Jeremiah.

CONCLUSION

The faith which God expects of anyone is commensurate with the revelation of Himself to an individual. Its justifying features of trust, honor, glorification of God, and recognition of His goodness, are enjoyed by both Jews of old and disciples of Christ. The people of covenant throughout the ages have had the benefit of the specially revealed Scripture, the fullest expression of the mind and will of God. Additionally, Gentiles though lacking special biblical revelation were doing what is right, maintaining a measure of authentic faith. These trusting sheep indeed know God and possess a fund of truth obeyed from the heart. None is alone in a foreign pasture bereft of his Shepherd's guidance.

The only defensible conclusion is that all righteous people who love God stand justified by belief in Him, whether living before or after the cross, novice or elder, in or out of a formal covenant with God. The "whoevers" and the "everys" of Romans 2:6-13 show that *all* who do good enjoy a right relationship with God.

And so, when Christian evangelists meet a God-fearer who possesses positive behavioral characteristics like those of Cornelius, they should tell him God's way more accurately, to wit: faith in Jesus as the Christ and the importance of baptism. Acts 10:2, 22, 35, 43 and 11:7 clearly point to a highly favored man of God who was eager to follow his Creator in all ways. He was a sheep not of the covenantal fold who had to be gathered in. Cornelius was accountable to the truths of God only as exposed to them and assimilated them into his *epignosis*—an understanding mind (see Chapter Five). In no sense was he destined for judgment.

Righteous Cornelius is comparable to Apollos, a learned man described as "instructed in the way of the Lord…fervent in spirit…speaking and teaching accurately the things concerning Jesus." (Acts 18:24-26). He was evidently not lost before Priscilla and Aquila took him aside, just not fully enlightened. But Apollos needed to be schooled in God's way more accurately toward greater truth (v. 26)—to make him better—and so did Cornelius by Peter. Among moral people experiencing only naturally revealed truths about God, what joy there must be when they finally encounter the superior light of Jesus as it enters their lives.

Similarly, by Peter coming to Joppa, Cornelius escaped having to continue his journey through life in the lesser light of general revelation. His prayers to for greater enlightenment ascended on high, and Peter came and shared Jesus with Him, thus allowing him to perceive more perfectly than ever before the full light of God.

In salvation history it has always been the same. Everyone among the Gentiles working righteousness and respecting God is saved by grace through faith. And if any of these might have the opportunity to perfect their faith by embracing Christ, to make it better, they must seek and accept "words by which you will be saved." Let us ever be truth seekers who after receiving and obeying additional words of truth can rightfully exclaim, "I have believed!"

CHAPTER SEVEN

◇◇◇◇◇◇◇◇◇◇◇◇◇◇◇

THE HALLMARK OF A RELATIONSHIP WITH GOD: SEEKING, NOT REJECTING, TRUTH

The manner in which anyone responds to understood truth is fundamental to a proper relationship with God. Denying truth by suppressing it in unrighteousness brings forth divine displeasure (see Chapter Two), but the truth-seeker who maintains a disposition of hungering and thirsting for righteousness displays the positive attitude God desires from everybody (Matt. 5:5). Ezra 8:22 declares that "God's hand is upon all who seek Him for good," those who openly approach the way of right without bias and sincerely yearn for everything that is right. With noble intent they never knowingly disregard even the slightest bit of reality. In response, God gives such people protection, acceptance.

On his second missionary journey, Paul on Mars Hill told the citizens of Athens that "they should seek God, in the hope that they might feel their way toward Him and find Him" (Acts. 17:27). This lofty endeavor is the very essence of truth seeking. As the offspring of the living Creator and bearing His likeness (Gen. 1:27), man was created capable of knowing God and yearning for Him, inasmuch as the evidence of God exists within and around everyone (Rom. 1:19). Thus, seeking God is rooted in the creation itself, as well as in the mind of every man.

A proper approach to truth is therefore crucial, for John 3:21 declares that "he who does what is true comes to the light." Conversely, "Everyone who does evil hates the light, and does not come to the light" (v. 20). All living righteously through an affirmative response to available light show that their works are wrought by God (v. 21b). The light also reveals the wickedness of the depraved and restless, ultimately forcing such people into deeper darkness or perhaps a change of life.

Metaphorically, this light specifically refers to the fact that the God of heaven in the fullness of time disclosed Himself through His son Jesus (John 1:14, Heb. 1:1-2) as the ultimate expression of God's mind and will. Significantly, this light (*Logos*) fully embraces all eternal truths which have been accorded to covenant people through special revelation, the Scriptures, as well as manifestations of God to all through general revelation—the external creation and internally in man's sense of ought. Thus, a measure of moral reality is evident in everyone regardless of time or culture.

All people have a degree of truth and reality *in* them and can generally recognize good and evil because it is accessible *to* them (Rom. 1:19). This is their available light. Divine Reason (the *Logos* of John 1) enlightens one and all, enabling truth-seekers regardless of time or location to accept the ultimate Light if it were made available to them. All who deny the light and truth by choosing to remain in darkness will have the retribution of God continually pouring forth upon them (Rom. 1:18). As developed in Chapter One, such people "do not honor Him as God nor give thanks" (v. 21). These are the first steps into pernicious degradation and wickedness (vv. 22-32).

The immoral do not stand condemned for *rejecting* Christ's gospel for they may have never had access to it, or for lacking a covenant with God, but for *suppressing* what natural truths they currently comprehend: God's creative work in nature and faithfulness to living up to understood ethical principles. From observation and reason (Rom. 1:20), everybody can become aware of God's righteousness, glory, power, benevolence, wisdom, and the orderliness of nature (see Chapter Two).

The Gentile, created like the Jew as "very good" and in God's likeness (Gen. 1:27), is obligated to respond to available manifestations of truth, for they are his gospel and will serve as the basis for acceptance. Since he has not entered into a formal covenant with God, such a person is not accountable for unknown specially revealed prophetic and apostolic truths of Scripture. He cannot *reject* what he has not *heard*. Such an outsider is nevertheless accountable for the reality of the Creator and adhering to moral goodness. Living by the dictates of conscience is his "law" (see Chapter Five). After all, if anyone embraces all of the truth he can possibly find, what more could a merciful God expect of him?

In every generation since the cross, various people have been guiltlessly ignorant of gospel truths, yet they have followed God's will as known and regulated through the dictates of conscience. These "excused" (Rom. 2:14) faithful have access to the hope of eternal life. Would the God of equity bar access to heaven people who have maintained a clear conscience and striven to attain and embrace knowledge of the Creator, though they lack exposure to Scripture revelation?

Sincerity does matter if it involves honest truth seeking. God judges by the heart all who seek Him wholeheartedly (I Sam. 16:7, Acts 8:37), with full strength and understanding. He maintains fellowship, in every era and in all places, with all who love Him and embrace all understood truths. A fair and just God does not ask for more.

Evidently, faith is not so much a matter of believing and obeying a check list of Bible doctrines as it is maintaining a truth-seeking heart and an honest approach toward all of life's situations. Faith in Romans 2-4 points to a sincere yearning after the true God, and a humble obedient spirit in doing His will to the extent that it is known. Paul wrote to the Philippians, "Only whereunto we have attained, by that same rule, let us walk" (3:16). Everyone is thus obligated to live in conformity to the knowledge possessed—the teaching God has committed to him.

Throughout life, all Christians exist in various stages of growth, living by their current understanding of truth (II Peter 1:12). They walk in the light (I John 1:7) at a particular level of knowledge of right and wrong. It is the same with non-covenant Gentiles as well. They live according to the truth gained through seeking God in nature and recognizing evil and living morally. Such people also possess the spirit of faith (see Chapter Eight).

IGNORANCE AND THE TRUTH

Cultivating a truth-seeking disposition—a desire to know God and doing well—is far more important than recognizing specific Bible commandments and letter-obeying them. John 7:17 touches upon intent and motivation: "If any man's will is to do His will, he shall know the teaching..." People who hunger and thirst for righteousness, and maintain a disposition to act upon known truths, are the delight of the God of heaven. He will always have fellowship with such ones, however unaware of multiplied revealed Bible teachings.

Not all ignorance is the same. All are born innocent and lack knowledge "just of different things," as Will Rogers once said. In contrast, willful ignorance stems from an unwillingness to seek, accept, and live by truth (cp. II Peter 3:5). Such an attitude is not innocent, and will surely condemn, for it stems from habitual suppression of truth (Rom. 1:18, cp. Prov. 1:25).

Therefore, ignorance of itself does not bring sin or guilt. If it did, no one could be saved. Nor does knowledge save. As Paul stated, "Knowing puffs up, but love edifies. If anyone imagines that he knows something, he does not yet know as he ought to know" (I Cor. 8:1-3; see also 3:18). If anyone depends upon knowledge to be justified before God, he does not yet know well enough how to be righteous.

Some counter this conclusion by declaring that all ignorance damns, citing Paul's response to the philosophers of Mars Hill in Athens: "The times of ignorance God overlooked, but now he commands all men everywhere to repent" (Acts 17:30). But this ignorance did not relate to general repentance, as explained in

Chapter Thirteen, Section Eleven; it was specifically aimed at Grecian idolaters (v. 16). The apostle countered this state of mind by telling them how to gain a relationship with the true God of heaven by covenanting with him in the gospel.

Paul treated his truth-seeking audience as ignorant worshipers whom God had not condemned, not as willful transgressors of heavenly ways. He had heretofore simply overlooked their sin. Paul's mild tone of speech befitted a non-condemnatory educational presentation, unlike the tongue-lashing institutional Jews received from Stephen, who perceived insincerity and hypocrisy on their part (Acts 7:51-53; cp. Matt. 23:13-36). Because of the information Paul supplied to the Athenians, they became responsible for their idolatry and were required to repent. At that point they would be responsible for additional truths taught them; intentional dismissal of new information would result in condemnation.

Belief is based upon evidence—data—and without it there can be no faith. Therefore, there are general distinctions between unbelief, disbelief, and the lack of belief. Jesus compassionately helped a belief that is weak (Mark 9:24). When anyone *refuses* to believe evidence presented to him, that is disbelief (Mark 16:14). One who hears and deliberately rejects knowledge after understanding it is lost.

In contrast, the ignorant unbeliever cannot choose to reject additional truth. There is no condemning guilt when a person is unavoidably unknowing of certain truths or facts. He cannot "disbelieve" what he does not know, what he is unaware of. Therefore, a crucial distinction exists between a heart which does not accept the gospel because he has never heard it, and one who having received the good news about Jesus deliberately casts it aside.

At the end-time judgment, responsibility to know and obey various truths will be measured according to ability and opportunity, well-established biblical principles. There will be no condemnation for disobedience when a lack of occasion to adhere to commands was not possible. In the matter of contributing to the poor, God holds an individual responsible only for what he can give (II Cor. 8:12). In a famous parable, the master dispensed talents "in proportion to every man's ability" (Matt. 25:15)—what he was capable of doing or producing—and he would not be accountable for more in the absence of talents to do more.

In the parable of the sower, good seed planted in various soils brought forth yields of a hundred-fold, sixty-fold, and thirty-fold. But all of these good hearts pleased the sower, for each produced what he could (Matt: 13:4-23; Luke 8:4-15). Apparently the more knowledge and ability one possesses, the more he is responsible to God, a principle fully in accord with James 4:17: "To him that knows to do good, and does it not, to him it is sin."

Any increase in knowledge, opportunity, and ability heightens responsibility toward God. In Luke 12:47-48, Jesus discussed various kinds of servants. The unprepared and disobedient would be beaten with many lashes, while the ignorant (who did things worthy of receiving lashes) would receive far less punishment. Significantly, Jesus then added, "From everyone who has been given much, that much will be demanded; and from the one who has been entrusted with much [more], much more will be asked" (v. 48b). Judgment is meted out in proportion to opportunities and gifts enjoyed, and man's response to their mandate.

As Jesus sent out the twelve disciples and the seventy to preach the gospel of the kingdom to the Jews (Matt. 10:4-42, Luke 10:1-20), he again spoke of responsibility for hearing and obeying truth. Jesus declared that those Jews in such places as Capernaum, Korazin and Bethsaida (Matt. 11:21-26) who refused to respond to his teaching, would be worse off than the inhabitants of Sodom and Gomorrah. Their judgment would be more tolerable than for the Jews of Jesus' day because those ancient cities lacked the same opportunity to hear God's message (Gen. 19:23-26). Thus, some of their citizens might still have hope of salvation, as well as those in Jesus' day living in the Gentile towns of Tyre and Sidon (Luke 10:15).

Although God had to physically destroy sinful Sodom (Jude 7), the Jews who heard the disciples' preaching about Jesus would be held more accountable than people in that ancient city. Unrepentant Jews who did not welcome Jesus' disciples would not receive sympathy at the judgment, for in their spiritual inhospitableness they lightly esteemed the gospel by *rejecting* it. These people of the covenant should have been prepared to receive the truth, but would be lost because they deliberately chose not to believe in Jesus by *accepting* him.

Evidently, God is pleased to see honest seekers of right, people of integrity who respect Him and display a willingness to act responsibly to known moral principles. These are always heard and blessed by God (Acts 13:16, 26, 50; 16:14; 17:4, 17; 18:7). Acts 10-11 presents devout Cornelius, a God-fearer who prayed to the one true God continually, whose requests had ascended as a memorial before heaven, and God protected him (vv. 2-3). Peter later concluded after interacting with Cornelius that all of the morally right who respect the Creator are favored in the court of heaven (see Chapter Six).

Some teachers assert that God does not hear the prayers of a sinner, citing John 9:31, but even in this instance they alter the intent of an uninspired formerly blind man's statement. Jesus had touched him and had given him sight. Hauled before the Sanhedrin, a body of legalistic Jews which staunchly held that Jesus was a sinner, the man contended that since God "heard" Jesus and through Him had opened his eyes, he had to be a man highly favored, "for God does not hearken to sinners but to those who worship him and do his will." Therefore, the man actually intended to show that God deals directly with all who honestly seek Him.

Scripture is silent about God *not* answering the prayers of people living outside of the covenant yet abiding in their present truth.

Soon afterward, Jesus supplied the healed man with information so that he might believe. He said, "It is for judgment I came into the world, that those who do not see may see, and those with sight may become blind" (John 9:39). When the Pharisees inquired angrily, "Are we also blind? "the Master retorted: "If you were blind, you would have no guilt; but now that you say 'We see', your guilt remains" (v. 41; cp. 1 Cor. 3:18).

Note the spiritual equation: blind to truth equals no guilt, no sin. A person who does not know a truth is not responsible for it (John 15:22, 24). Conversely, when anyone hears and understands (see Chapter Two), he is accountable, and sins when he transgresses truth, as did the Pharisees of John 9:40-41. In comprehending and refusing to accept the teaching, such a one stands condemned (II Thess. 1:8, 1 Pet. 4:17).

Jesus also had these critical distinctions in mind when he said, "If I had not come and spoken to them, they would not have had sin, but now they have no excuse for their sin" (John 15:22-24). His words and doing good among them made the difference; thereafter they were under sin for rejecting the truth of Jesus as Christ and not before.

Paul agreed, stating, "Where there is no law, there is no transgression" (Rom. 4:15). To be responsible to a law one must understand it and be amenable to that law. Light (truth) brings responsibility to do good (Jas. 3:1).

HUNGERING AND THIRSTING
AFTER RIGHTEOUSNESS

Approaching the light and seeking truth is the essence of God-acceptance, and should humble everyone, making them aware of their own fallibility, ignorance, inadequacies, and failures. While lack of effort is inexcusable, no man of any era or circumstance can fully live up to his understanding of God's ways for "all fall short" (Rom. 3:23). Adhering to doctrinal truths sustains no direct relationship to salvation; that is why it is by grace through faith (Rom. 4:16, Eph. 2:8-9). Dressed in Jesus' righteousness alone, we have been forgiven and rescued by the one who is truth personified (Col. 1:12; Eph. 1:7-8, 4:32). Indeed, Jesus is our righteousness (I Cor. 1:30; cp. Phil. 3:9).

Nobody is presently regarded as good merely through adhering to morality and obtaining Bible knowledge, and keeping commandments. Everyone is imperfect and stands guilty of sin. Even a truth-seeking attitude is not enough. The avenue of salvation has always been by way of Jesus, for he is the way, the truth, and the life for all people, whether in or out of a formal covenant with God. Experiencing death for all men (Heb. 2:9), Jesus' blood potentially covers the sins of the whole world (I John 2:1-2).

Everyone throughout time who would attain eternal life does so because of Jesus' death on the cross. There are no exceptions. His blood covers the transgressions of all honest seekers of truth and righteousness and lovers of God who continually trust in Him, even those ignorant of his agency. The blood of Christ flowed backward to the people of Israel in Old Testament times, covering their sins (Rom. 3:24-26; Heb. 9:15-16, 11:39-40), and also to righteous Gentiles in the Egyptian-Babylonian-Roman world, even though none of them specifically knew that God would provide through His son the vital covenant way of being cleansed.

Similarly, Jesus' blood covers the transgressions of those who respect God in this era after the cross, people who never have been exposed to apostolic teachings, yet earnestly seek God, "groping to find Him" (Acts 17:27). Such honest, sincere hearts may live without ever entering into formal covenant with God, yet through Christ's blood there is cleansing and forgiveness. God knows their hearts and accounts for their lack of special covenant revelation.

Pious, sincere people limited to general revelation embedded in conscience, nevertheless can possess the spirit of faith, even if it lacks the specific instruction which covenanters have access to because they have the greater light embodied in Scripture. When these doers of good search after what is right, the eternal Father is continually mindful of their truth-seeking attitude.

While en route to Corinth and preaching the gospel on his second missionary journey, Paul was told by God's Spirit that "the Lord hath many people in this city" (Acts 18:9-10). In that Grecian community there were various Gentiles seeking God and His truth, possessing the spirit of faith. Now God wanted them to hear the gospel of Christ and bring them further along toward all truth and make their souls better, enhancing their election (see Chapter Six).

Would a fair and just God have consigned these good hearts among the Corinthians to hell for failure to hear the gospel? Who is so bold to assign them to Satan's domain? Paul numbered uncircumcised truth-seekers among the spiritually circumcised (Rom. 2:26-29). Those Corinthians were part of God's elect, for He explicitly called them "my people."

As with Christians, these Corinthian God-fearers in some way sought after righteousness. They were not "liars, idolaters, thieves murderers, etc." (I Cor. 6:9-10). These righteous ones were not wronging or injuring others. Positive natural truth in all honest seekers of right leads to honoring the Creator in moral living where there is an awareness of sin in transgressing the conscience. Nobody is made right by perfunctorily performing good works in an attempt to satisfy this hungering and thirsting. Rather, the *thirst itself* is a revelation of the righteousness of Christ, and is a demonstration of the truth-seeker's intent and disposition to do God's will. Living a life of faith is what makes such people eternally secure in a relationship with God.

All people of God must allow an educated faith to shine through to immerse their thoughts and prompt the spontaneous, natural performance of good works in response to God's will as understood. It is by that standard which God commands us to walk in (Phil. 3:16). Even then, there can be no claim to personal righteousness (3:9) or pleasing God through a system of doing good deeds (Eph. 2:8-9, Rom. 11:6).

CHAPTER EIGHT

THE SPIRIT OF FAITH
AND RIGHTEOUSNESS

In every place throughout time, the Spirit of faith in God transcends propositional or doctrinal religion, and it rests squarely on the concept of the available light, Natural Law. This Spirit is found in the good found throughout all nations and cultures, and bountifully exists among people of light who believe in God and practice righteousness, though they may not be connected with formal religion.

Long before he met Jesus, a certain Roman centurion exhibited this spirit, and it was the basis of his implicit trust in God (Matt. 8:5-13, Luke 7:1-10). He lived by the light of available truth, sincerity and high mindedness. Jesus marveled first at the patience of this man with a heart for God, and then at his depth of assurance in what Jesus could do for him. Concluding a simple request to heal his servant, the humble centurion confidently said, "If you just say the word..." To this strong measure of trust, Jesus responded, "I have not found so great faith as this, not even in Israel"—the people of the covenant (Luke 7:9).

The centurion's faith was not in self-reliance but in simple assurance in the power of Jesus to make a difference. This is the kind of faith that Jesus continually looked for during the course of his ministry. It is the faith that justifies, whenever or wherever it is found. It is a conviction that makes one right with God, and is based on the amount of understanding and knowledge (light) one has.

More than just baptized believers, righteous Gentiles unaware of the gospel can walk in newness of life and daily renewal through virtue, goodness, understanding, temperance, love, kindness to others, and godliness in faith, just as Christians are called to do (II Pet. 1:5-8). This is letting the Spirit of Christ richly dwell amid the good, the pure, the honorable, the upright and holy things as cataloged by Paul in Philippians 4:8. The truth of God is displayed in love, peace, patience, kindness, goodness, gentleness and other fruit of the Spirit (Gal. 5:22).

The goal for all who follow the promptings of God's law in the heart is to glorify and serve Him. Here, the spirit of Christ is active in a lofty plane of self-denial wherein dwells righteousness, justice, mercy, kindness, forgiveness, and tender-heartedness (see Eph. 4:32). By no means do Christians monopolize these universal virtues. Only the arrogant would claim that in the natural realm there is no spirit of mercy, forgiveness or saving faith. To the contrary, when anyone in any place strives for the improvement of fellow man by helping people to be honorable and just, God's Spirit is at work and salvation (acceptance) potentially can reside there.

The man of God in every place emulates the portraits of a righteous man found in Psalms 1 and 15. God constantly watches over the path of the upright. The follower of God is like a tree near a stream, bearing fruit in season. He walks in truth and love, avoiding living according to the flesh. He instead constantly seeks the Spirit (Rom. 8:13), living blamelessly, speaking the truth from the heart. Everyone with a merciful, forgiving spirit will not fail of God's mercy (Matt. 5:7, 6:14-15).

The Spirit of God resides amid people caring of the poor, the sick and imprisoned, helping the helpless, showing compassion, as explained by Jesus in Matthew 25:31-46 (see Chapter Ten). God's Spirit is in evidence where these are practiced, anytime and anywhere, from the time of Genesis onward, demonstrating God's saving justice as embodied in both Scripture and Natural Law.

All people leading virtuous lives through the power of the Spirit are justified and will receive at the final judgment the reward of acquittal. It is the positive, graceful standard by which God will judge both Christians and Gentiles. The standard at the future judgment centers upon a righteous life. The unwritten law in the heart administers universal justice and righteousness, and not the written Torah, the Jewish prophetic writings, or the New Testament.

Regardless of the manner in which God will receive good-hearted Gentiles, their right- standing ultimately comes through the life of Christ through his sacrifice at the cross. He is the fulfillment, the goal (Rom. 10:4) and purpose of law, and is the very embodiment of God's unwritten law through which all people everywhere can attain knowledge of good and evil, virtue and vice. Jesus' act of dying on behalf of all (Rom. 5:15-21) exemplifies heavenly justice through the Spirit of Christ and the universality of available light.

Throughout the heart of the Roman letter (3:21-6:23), Paul shows that the "law of the Spirit of Life in Christ Jesus" (8:4) is the means by which God delivers the captive from the power of sin. Neither devotion to Torah nor a structured law thought to be found in the New Testament can convey this vitality; rather, true justice and acceptability is found in a relationship with Christ Jesus, for we are saved by his life (5:10). It is he who brings saving justice and life to all men (5:18), through his righteousness, so that many are made upright (v. 19) as they walk imperfectly in their available light. What a redeemer! Jesus died for everyone, including the faithful abiding in the truths of Natural Law, for he is the savior of all men (I John 2:2, I Tim. 4:10).

JUSTIFICATION BY FAITH

A discussion of how faith justifies the moral people of God properly begins with the ancient patriarch Abraham, who believed in God, "and it was counted to him for righteousness" (Gen. 15:6). More than an exalted father among fellow patriarchs, Abraham would be the "father of a multitude," and his spiritual descendants would be as innumerable as the stars in the sky. The accepted would arise from "every tongue and tribe and people and nation" (Rev. 5:9, 7:9), people following present truth and benefiting from remission of sin through the blood of Christ. All are justified by faith, and that makes them sons of God (Gal. 3:27), placing them in His family.

In evidencing faith through love, the believer is born of God, as expressly stated in I John 4:7. In I John 5, the teaching is plain: "Whoever believes that Jesus is the Christ is a child of God" (v. 1) and such a one has overcome the world through faith (v. 4). Verse 5 states, "and who is the one who overcomes the world, but he who believes that Jesus is the Son of God." The very purpose of John's writings is to assure that believers may know that they have eternal life (v. 13, John 20:31).

By extension the body of believers also includes righteous non-Christians following their present truth in Natural Law. I John 2:29 assures us that "all who *do what is right* have been born of Him." Romans 2 emphatically shows that all who persistently do good have excused consciences and are accorded "glory and honor and immortality, eternal life" (vv. 7, 9). In faithfulness these people are accepted of God by virtue of faith, and God respects them in every place and time, declaring that they are born of Him. There is no partiality with God (v. 10). Romans 2:26-29 shows that these Gentiles living in accordance with moral law are given the status of "circumcised people" in full equality with Christians in respect to acceptability before the heavenly throne.

Romans 3:21-4:15 develops the magnificent doctrine of justification by faith for covenanters and non-covenanters alike. Paul speaks of God's saving justice and how God accounts as righteous all who display active faith. Abraham is the star witness. God reckons righteousness apart from works (Rom. 4:4), and He is the One who forgives and covers sins. It is by believing not achieving. We are heirs of

God through that very righteousness (v. 13). The conclusion in verse 16 drives the truth home superlatively: the promise is to faith so that it comes as a free gift and is secure for all of Abraham's descendants. Through God's grace the promise is made *sure*; performance in systems of works can never be secure.

Galatians 3:6-14 reaffirms what is taught in Romans 3:21-4:16. Believers throughout the world are sons of Abraham (v. 7), who is the father of all God-fearers, both Christians and Gentiles. Righteousness is based on faith (Rom. 10:6). Romans 9:30 declares that untold numbers of Gentiles pursue a righteousness by faith and find it, a theme introduced in Romans 2:13-14 which states that through the law in the heart they have excused consciences. These righteous ones along with Christians have the blessing of forgiveness of sin made possible by the cross and the righteousness of Christ.

Comforted and enveloped by the blessings that come from faith, trust in God and heart-obedience, all believers in God everywhere can boldly venture forth blamelessly, fearing nothing. The modern concept of faith *in* Jesus does not save. Rather, salvation to one and all is by possessing a faith *like* his: confident, obedient, trusting and self-sacrificing.

Perhaps this is what is meant by Paul's statement "from faith to faith" (Rom. 1:17), a phrase which is immediately followed by a lengthy discussion of how the faith of moral Gentiles outside of formal covenant with God justifies (Rom 1:18-3:31). In particular, verse 3:25 declares that God presented to us Jesus "as a propitiation in his blood through faith," for he exacted forever the full payment for the sins of all of the righteous throughout time. This truth must ever burn in our hearts. This is the good news! This is the gospel of Christ!

THE RIGHTEOUSNESS OF GOD

Front and center in any discussion of Natural Law and walking in available light is the saving justice of God. Romans 3:21-31 is the basic text. Through Torah came knowledge of sin, but now apart from law God's righteousness has been revealed to all believers in every place. Jesus Christ is the goal of the law for righteousness for everyone who believes (Rom. 10:4). Since all have sinned (Rom 3:23), God has supplied through His son the avenue of averting divine wrath for everyone.

I John 2:2 plainly relates that Jesus Christ the righteous "is the sacrifice to expiate our sins, and not only ours [Christians], but also those of the whole world." This statement of propitiation or gift offering transcends time and localities. John further declared that everyone who loves God might have life through His son (I John 4:7-9). Verily, God sent His son "to be the expiation for our sins" (v. 10).

Romans 3:25 shows that through Jesus' offering of himself, the propitiation,

God has simply forgiven and forgotten the sins of the righteous in the Old Testament era. The cross is the means by which sins were paid for on behalf of *all* believers everywhere throughout time (see above). The author of Hebrews further shows how God reconciled Himself to man: "It behooved him [Christ] in all things to be made like unto his brethren, that he might be a merciful and faithful high priest in things pertaining to God, to make propitiation for the sins of the people" (Heb. 2:17).

Paul's words explain why tradition's special pleading of exclusive passages such as John 14:6 "I am the way the truth and the life" and "there is salvation in no other name" (Acts 4:12), do not negate God's acceptance of the present-day moral righteous, believers under Natural Law outside of the Christian fold. Indeed, these passages emphasize that it is only through the *power* of Jesus Christ (Acts 4:7, 10) and the cross that *anyone's* salvation, anytime and anywhere, is actualized as they walk in their present truth, whether under moral law or truth furnished by Scripture.

God's demonstration of saving justice (Rom. 3:26) and justification by faith extends to both Jew and Gentile (v. 29), the circumcised and uncircumcised by their faith. This comports with verses 2:25-29, wherein Gentiles obeying moral law are given the status of "circumcised people," and are on a par with faithful Christians and have informally covenated with God. Indeed, these uncircumcised following their available light (truth) in righteous living are far better off than baptized believers who consistently and purposefully fail to do His will. Verse 29 completes the thought: the man approved of God, that is saved, "is the one who is inwardly a Jew [a person of covenant], and real circumcision is of the heart, which is something not of the letter but the spirit."

Everyone—Christians this side of the cross, the covenant Jews of old and pure-hearted Gentiles in an any era—benefits from the righteousness of God and the propitiation made possible by Jesus' once for all offering of himself on the cross. For one and all salvation is by grace through faith, and the faith that God expects coincides with the revelation of God known to each individual, their available light. Here indeed is the universal sufficiency of God's saving grace; it is freely given impartiality, not only to Christians but also to righteous moral God-fearers. Here, the justice of God is robustly displayed.

Our benevolent God has a purpose for His creation. He is a God of self-disclosure and wants to share Himself with us. We bear His image and have value. To one and all God has not left Himself without witness (Acts 14:17). Everyone who has ever lived is accountable for how he has handled the light accorded him, the truth made available to him.

To his covenanted ones, God's will has been conveyed not only in Natural Law but also in special biblical revelation. God constantly shows all-embracing concerns for His created, through the systematic moral universe, the vast realm of nature. David of old asked, "Where can I go from your Spirit," realizing that His hand should ever lead him on paths of right in every circumstance of life (Psa. 139:1-4). In any of these ways God has provided information for which men are accountable. Though in Adam all die, all are made alive in Christ (I Cor. 15:22; see also Rom. 5:17-19). Mercy has been extended to all (Rom. 11:32).

Salvation is intimately connected with God's love, His righteousness and justice. These are the foundation of His throne (Psa. 89:14, 97:2). Isaiah 45:21 identifies the Creator as a "righteous God and Savior." From all the nations, the Father wishes to draw to Him people of faith and goodness wherever the may be, as shown in various parables of Christ, such as those in Matthew 25 and Luke 15. As the redeemer, God desires that the world would be saved through His son, and did not commission him to condemn the world (John 3:17).

CHAPTER NINE
◇◇◇◇◇◇◇◇◇◇◇◇◇◇

SALVATION AND JUDGMENT

The Bible in many ways defines an on-going positive relationship with God. Though salvation is a word frequently associated with entrance into heaven after death, it much more often refers to a present acceptable state of covenant fellowship with God. It is a current, immediate blessing for believers, anywhere and at any time.

Salvation is a deliverance from sin and its consequences. The New Testament contains scores of descriptive words and phrases which describe this blessed relationship with God. Saved people hunger and thirst for righteousness, display mercy and forgiveness, love others, and desire the will of the Father. They do good things for fellow man, practice self control and separate themselves from sinful situations, obeying God from the heart. The good conduct of both covenanters and righteous Gentiles shows that God is with them.

Respecters of the creation and the moral order demonstrate moral excellence, self-control, godliness, and righteousness in all humility. These virtues are not exclusively the attributes of Christians, for moral people among the residue of humanity display them as well, and God takes note of them, comforting and saving them. By adhering to their available light, they are a justified people reverencing God. They are devout as were the Jews on Pentecost and Cornelius (See Chapter Six).

Throughout time the accepted ones accounted righteous under Natural Law are "many" and in the cause of righteousness are numbered with Christians (Matt. 8:11, cp. Luke 13:29). The throng is as innumerable as the sands of the sea, consisting of "thousands upon thousands, ten thousand times ten thousands" arising from every tongue and country (Gen. 22:17, 15:5, 26:4). Revelation 5:9 and 7:9 show that the extent of the saved by the blood of Christ are an unnumbered host, a multitude, and cumulatively show universality. These countless redeemed ones come without distinction of race, geographical location or religious orientation—in fact from all conceivable backgrounds. But someone might ask, what about the "few" Jesus said would enter by the narrow gate to life (Matt. 5:13). In response, see chapter Thirteen, Section Six.

Of all the people who have ever lived, there is a distinct class of individuals that cannot be saved. All who disbelieve in the existence of the Creator, the evil people whose deeds are of the flesh, and those who knowingly reject the truth of the gospel of Christ, are the ones God turns away at the judgment. "Salvation is far from the wicked: for they seek not your will" (Psa. 119:155). These people do not develop a relationship with God and will perish, undergo the second death. They are the "chaff which shall be burned up" (Matt. 3:12).

A mind set on the flesh also characterizes people who staunchly adhere to the letter of Scripture, the legalist. Romans 7:7-25 shows that this is the antithesis of internal harmony with the spirit of Christ and virtue, the purity of goodness. The mind of the Spirit follows the intent of God through faith. His law is on the heart as he follows whatever light is available to him. They move up in obedience as additional light of God shines on their hearts. They embrace truth wherever it is found and do not intentionally reject it.

Jesus as the ultimate goal of the law (Rom. 10:4) exemplifies the quality of justice that approaches universal true-life moral goodness. Romans 5:18-19 decisively shows that it was "one man's act of righteousness" on the cross that leads to justification and life for all, covenanters and non-covenanters alike; it was through his obedience the many are righteous (see Chapter Eight). Jesus was submissive to the will and purposes of God apart from the written Torah, serving as a model for God's people today who follow His will as understood, the moral light which is engraved on their hearts.

The wicked are not so, for they cast aside the truth. In Acts 8:22, Peter told the wayward brother Simon to repent of his wickedness. Various sinning brothers need to be restored (Gal. 6:1) and brought back to their first love (Rev. 2:4-5, cp. Jas. 5:19-20). Others in their evil passions and desires have crucified the Son of God again (Heb. 6:6), and thus are lost, numbered among the wicked. In no uncertain terms Hebrews 10:26-27 condemns willful sin. These examples apply to people who have heard the truth and accepted it. In contrast, all who have never had an opportunity to hear and believe will be judged by the measure of spiritual light they have encountered during their lifetimes.

In short, Jesus died for everyone. His mission was "to seek and to save that which was lost" among the covenant Jews (Luke 19:10). He "came into the world to save sinners" (I Tim. 1:5). He "came not to judge the world, but to save the world" (John 12:47). His charge was not *only* "to rescue his people [Israel] from their sins" (Matt. 1:21), but also to save non-covenanters as well. In I John 4:14, the apostle wrote that "we have seen and do testify that the Father sent the Son to be the Savior of the world." See also I John 2:2.

The teaching could not be plainer: many right-hearted people though lacking a formal covenant with God and Scripture instruction, nevertheless possess a present accepted relationship with God through the Lord Jesus Christ. These many with the law in the heart also are a part of God's called out from a world of darkness, the invisible worldwide church whose head is invisible (John 1:18, I Tim. 6:16; cp. Col. 1:15, Luke 17:21). God is the savior of the entire human race, but His special people today are believes in Christ (I Tim. 4:10).

MAN IS NOT THE JUDGE

Tradition insists that everyone today not in the Christian fold without exception will spend eternity in hell. They say that no mercy or grace will be accorded righteous, God-seekers faithfully adhering to Natural Law because they have not submitted to the gospel of Christ. To them it is unfortunate for the untold millions of good hearts who will die without ever having a chance to hear the good news. The law of the gospel must not be minimized, it is insisted.

On its face this conclusion appears to exhibit a narrowly focused, legalistic concept of judgment and righteousness. Scripture makes it clear that "God so loved the world" (John 3:16), not just the Westernized, literate portions of it who have access to Bibles, and that He does not wish "for any to perish, but for all to come to repentance" (v. 17, cp. II Pet. 3:9). He desires that every person arrive at a saving knowledge of His will by responding to available truth. The question is, has God made provision for this? Have other moral God-fearers been given opportunity? Or is salvation only for those fortunate very, very few who through circumstances were born in areas of the world where the preaching of Christ is regularly heard and Bibles are available? If the latter is true, then millions of moral people are regrettably predestined for wrath after the judgment, through no fault of their own.

Tradition counters this conundrum by advancing some sort of "providentially preserved theory." It argues that God foreknows who is searching for Him and thus He will spare the life of such a one until an evangelist can track him down and eventually enter his life to tell him about Christ. God would somehow prolong the lives of both the preacher and the one untaught, granting safety to both, to finally interact in the gospel. Adherents improperly cite as examples the evangelist Philip seeking the Ethiopian eunuch (Acts 8:27-39) and Peter to Cornelius (Acts 10-11).

This emotionally toned theory is not realistic. In fact, in the last two millennia of time millions of God-fearing moral people from every tongue and nation who genuinely yearn to know the Creator, have in fact gone to the grave never hearing about the gospel of Christ. Jesus himself told his disciples that many honest hearts bearing good fruit will go unreached by saying, "The harvest is plenteous, but the laborers are few" (Luke 10:2). In other words, thousands of good hearts unexposed to the gospel message but adhering to the moral law to the best of their ability nevertheless possess ready, submissive dispositions, and would accept the gospel of Christ, if they could only come in contact with it. These good hearts will go unreaped because of the small number of available evangelists. The abundant harvest does not consist of lost persons, as tradition assumes. To the contrary, farmers associate the word "harvest" with a cash crop, not useless vegetation or weeds ultimately to be discarded.

How could the Judge in heaven exhibit equity, fairness, and righteousness, if He routinely consigned to eternal damnation ethical believers who have never heard the good name of Christ but nevertheless grope for him and desire opportunities to seek Him? There is a far more biblical position, namely that all people everywhere are responsible for the light accorded them and will ultimately be judged by the manner in which they handle that measure of natural moral truth. By willfully rejecting they are cast off, while others are saved and presently accepted by God by genuinely responding to their available light in fullness of faith. This view is consistent with the nature and character of the Judge who will decide fairly and benevolently the ultimate eternal fate of all.

Through many ways God has made Himself known to everyone in every place in all the ages, though methods have varied dramatically. In past times God revealed His will though dreams, visions, and direct revelations to His prophets. God has been disclosed to everyone in nature and the moral order. He also set forth truth through his servants the prophets. And He speaks most perfectly through the plan of redemption embodied in the person of His son, Jesus Christ (John 1:14, Heb. 1:1-2). God continually dispenses light, although some shines more brightly than others, and is thus more easily discerned.

This may be regarded as the progressive light under Natural Law, wherein at any stage in a lifetime people are responsible for following tenets currently understood, walking in the light of known understanding (II Peter 1:12) and not in darkness (I John 1:5). With each successive disclosure of Himself, further truth becomes evident, with Jesus as the pinnacle of revelation of eternal light (John 8:12).

Those blessed with the knowledge of the truth of Christ should seek opportunity to share it with neighbors who are currently under the guidance of lesser light. After all, if we in America enjoy the blessings of, say, electricity and running water to houses, should we not wish to improve the lot of people elsewhere living in primitive conditions? Similarly, Christians do not communicate spiritual blessings because of fear that good-hearted people might perish without them, but do so because they will prosper all the more by embracing the truth of Jesus. It is an effort to ennoble their lives, to bring them greater spiritual prosperity than ever before. It is not so much that we lead them to salvation as we enrich them with heavenly truths, thus upgrading their standing with God.

KNOWING AND EXPERIENCING GOD

God as Sovereign may choose the manner of saving anyone consistent with His righteousness. Who would argue against this? A loving God searches all hearts. His judgments are altogether righteous, for He will not judge everyone by a standard unknown to them. People familiar with God's revelation but disregard the evidence of His creation and the moral order, would also reject the truth of the gospel if it were presented to them. (see John 3:21). There is no difference in principle between the various hearts who cast off God, only in the brightness of light not accepted. Similarly, good hearts in fellowship with God and embracing His light differ in the measure of light possessed.

The essential question is: has a person lived up to his present understanding of the ways of God? Ecclesiastes 3:11 states that God has placed a present awareness of eternity in each of us. It is within everyone to seek God, and He would not have placed this impulse in man without also supplying the provision for light to fulfill it. Some are blessed with a small but distinct measure of moral consciousness and in recognition of the Creator. Christians in formal covenant with God are subject to these, and also possess the additional light of Jesus and his teaching, as preserved in the New Testament. Paul wrote of a general principle and gradation of responsibility, stating, "Let us keep on living by that same standard to which we have attained" (Phil. 3:16). There is a raising of the bar throughout our lifetimes.

God indeed takes note when people unaware of Christ live up to their current understanding of truth. They join Christians in maintaining grounds for hope in God's mercy by recognizing the true, the right, the virtuous. Paul taught that it is not those who merely *hear* God's law who will be saved, but those who *do* the law (Rom. 2:6-9). If they obey "by nature,"(v. 14), then it is by this principle they will be judged.

Men stand *accused* if they do not follow what they know about God. They are indeed accountable to that extent. On the other hand, they stand *excused* by faithfully adhering to light possessed. Paul in II Corinthians 8:12 taught this principle with regard to benevolence: "For if the willingness of mind is present, it is acceptable according to what a man has, not according to what he does not have." Therefore, all must abide by what is known, what they have to work with, as expressed by Jesus himself in the parable of the talents.

Every person faithfully following available truth has life and fellowship with God, acceptance, salvation. Every person not living according to understood truth is given time to repent (cf. Rev. 2:21), and God will not summarily bar the gate to salvation anyone for not having the opportunity to specifically hear of Christ. Commenting on Romans 1:20, early American restoration preacher Moses Lard stated, "Paul here assumes the great and constantly recurring fact in the divine government, that knowledge of duty is the measure of responsibility. Had the Gentiles [of Paul's day] not known, they would have been free, but having light, they were without excuse."

If God expects all men to grope for Him and find Him, and indeed He does, surely He has provided the *means* to know Him. God will judge every man according to how he has handled opportunities in life. This constitutes the basis of responsibility under heaven. In commenting upon Romans 1:18-25, the *Pulpit Commentary* states, "These words describe the condition of those who reject light from the standpoint of Him who is the great Searcher of hearts. He makes no mistakes. He makes no uncharitable judgments. In His sight those to whom He has given light, and who have chosen to [deliberately] reject it, are 'without excuse.'" Though disobedient people understand a measure of truth, their behavior translates into improper responses to it. It is fair and just that God should cast them aside at the Great Judgment.

CHAPTER TEN

◇◇◇◇◇◇◇◇◇◇◇◇

THE TWO WAYS

T he prophet Isaiah sternly pronounced affliction upon all living upside down
in their morality. "Woe upon those who call evil good and good evil, who
substitute darkness for light and light for darkness" (Isa. 5:20). Throughout the
Proverbs, man is called to be righteous, honest and fair, to do good instead of evil.
These wise of Israel reproved those who would absolve the guilty and condemn
the right, for both are abhorrent to God (Prov. 2:21-22; 10:7; 11:3-12; 12:20, 22;
22:1, 29:1, 12, etc.). Moses taught, "Do not cause the death of the innocent or
upright, and do not acquit the guilty" (Exod. 23:7). It is never ethical to do evil in
order to achieve good.

The Psalmists plainly delineates the Two Ways and destinies of man, as in
Psalm 1:6, "The Lord knows the way of the righteous, but the way of the wicked
shall perish. "The righteous/wicked dichotomy also occurs in 7:9-11, 11:2-7,
14:4-6, 32:10-11, 34:15-22, 37:16-29, 75:10, 97:10-12, etc. The prophets also
admonished the people to distinguish between the holy and the profane (Ezek.
33:18, 18:5-13; Jer. 34:15, 36:7; cp. Deut. 30:15-20). This is a strong, consistent
theme throughout the Jewish Scriptures.

In the time between the Testaments, various writers in Judah continued
the theme of the Two Ways and the warring in the conscience. The *Testament of
Judah* describes twin spirits, one of truth and another of deceit. The spirit of the
understanding of the mind shows man's inclination toward either truth or error
(20:2); each is "written upon the hearts of men" (20:3), obviously paralleling
Romans 2:14-15. Both passages also make reference to the judgment day.

Early in the Christian era, the Qumran community's *Manual of Instruction* records that man may have either a spirit of truth or the spirit of error, as in the document "The War Between the Children of Light and the Children of Darkness." Here are themes found in John's gospel (1:4, 8:12). This and similar instruction, together with an abundance of Old Testament texts, became the basis for Christian ethics. Jesus himself said that God provides the sun and rain for both the good and evil people (Matt. 5:45), to the just and the unjust. From his store of goodness, the good man brings forth good, while the bad man renders evil (Matt. 12:35).

At the end-time judgment angels will separate the iniquitous from the righteous (Matt. 13:49). The contrasts which appear in Mark 3:4, Matthew 7:9-11, 7:24, 12:35, 13:41, 25:29, etc., go to the heart of Natural Law. The Gentiles of Tyre and Sidon recognized good and evil, for their hearts were in accord with moral principles (Matt. 11:21, cp. 10:15). Here, the senses must be trained for discernment (Heb: 5:14). I Peter 3:8-17 emphasizes being zealous for what is right, contrasting it with the wrong, by appealing to Psalm 34:12-16. We must do well (v. 11), eschewing the bad by inclining toward the good. Gentiles with a moral compass embrace concepts like just, right, unjust, and wrong, precisely as they unfold in the New Testament.

The earliest church fathers show intimate familiarity with the Two Ways of Natural Law. The author of the *Didache* discussed at length the Way of Life which is to love God and neighbor, and the Way of Death which is wickedness, false testimonies, duplicity, pretension, and many other foul deeds and actions. The *Didache*, written about 100 A.D., mirrors the thought and practice of the rapidly emerging institutional church. Justin Martyr, Irenaeus, Theophilus of Antioch, Clement of Alexandria, Origen, Eusebius and others all taught that moral law came from God to point everyone away from the wrong to the right. Various systems through history affirm autonomy and truthfulness and justice, and forbid murder, lying, stealing, and the like. Examples of note are the Code of Hammurabi, the moral teachings of Aristotle, Karl Marx's writings on ethics, and the "Code of Handsome Lake" devised by an American Seneca chief.

Various secular writings disdain profiting from the pain of the unfortunate, speaking cruel or bitter things, and avoiding magical arts, sorceries, lustful desires, idolatries, false testimonies, fraud, malice and scores of similar selfish, hurtful actions. Denunciation of malevolent acts is inherent in the universal natural order. Good and evil actions routinely occur among men in everyday discourse, and God continually praises and condemns these separate and apart from biblical instruction.

INHERITING THE KINGDOM

M atthew 25:31-46 indicates that those in God's kingdom are people of faith who feed and supply drink to the hungry and thirsty, assist the stranger along the way, care for the sick and imprisoned, and clothe the needy. Love expressed to others in these and similar ways is the core of faith for both righteous Christians and non-Christians alike, especially when offered in support of anyone undergoing difficulty. These brothers of the Lord in verse 41 are not merely found in the Christian experience. In this judgment scene, *all* of the nations come before the Lord Jesus, and as King he speaks well of the most insignificant of his brothers among all peoples.

Thus, when the nations are gathered before Jesus in judgment, those who reject and deny truths which had been conveyed to them, will be "without excuse" (Rom. 1:20). People from all tongues and countries may not have encountered the greater revelatory light which Christians benefit from, but a vast number of others were in possession of sufficient truth to perceive God's nature and will. All who live and die with that degree of light are included in "the least of these brothers of mine."

Charles Ellicott wrote about people who stand before Christ's judgment seat, stating, "They have acted from what seemed merely human affection towards merely human objects, and they are therefore rightly represented as astonished when they hear that they have, in their ministrations to the sons of men, been ministering to the Son of Man." When the Lord informed these helpful individuals from "the nations" that they had been providing acts of kindness and helpfulness toward others, they were assuredly serving the King as well.

Evidently, these righteous ones were living according to available light, understood truths which had been impressed upon their hearts the need to be loving and helping others among "the nations." In commenting on Matthew 25, the *Pulpit Commentary* states: "Those who had not heard the gospel had shown the law of love written in their hearts, and the King now shows to them the meaning of their deeds of love." These non-Christians are numbered among the blessed of God through an acceptable conscience.

Regrettably, sectarian Christians support the notion that on the day of judgment, the Lord God might inquire about which "acts of worship" were employed in the Sunday assembly, the number of cups on the Lord Supper table, whether or not saints shared common meals in a church building, what was specifically supported out of the church treasury, and other artificial "weighty matters." These reflect an improper focus on what truly counts: loving God and neighbor, being zealous of good works, and doing the good and not evil. None of these human devices affect present salvation and eternal destiny, unless pressed to the point of division. Only then would it become a "weighty matter."

Instead, according to Matthew 25, judgment will be rendered according to how people behave toward others, recognizing needs and filling them. Service to fellow man is not defined by profession of religion, a creed, or participation in ceremonial acts of public worship. In verses 37-40, Jesus focused squarely on moral relationships and conduct, such as how one treated his brothers in specific deeds of kindness, love, displays of mercy, and compassion. "Whoever has the world's goods and beholds his brother in need and closes his heart against him, how can the love of God be remaining in him?" asked John (I John 3:17).

Whether or not a part of organized religion, God shines on the faithful who help, encourage, uplift and support others, and would withdraw favor from judgmental faultfinders and exclusivists who engender discord or fail to assist a neighbor. Responses to the questions raised by Jesus in Matthew 25:41-46 will help determine whether one will be counted among sheep or be found surrounded by goats on God's great Day of Decision.

CHAPTER ELEVEN

ACCENTUATING MERCY

N atural Law is structured similarly to God's future rewards and punishments, in that there are degrees of accountability, whether reward or punishment, which in turn are based on opportunity, enlightenment and revelation. Every person is responsible only for what light has been given to him, an eternal principle. The two-talent man's limitations were not like that of the five-talent man's, with whom God had entrusted more. As Jesus stated, "From everyone who has been given much shall much be required; and to whom they entrusted much, of him they will ask all the more" (Luke 12:48b). The apostle Paul declared that a person is judged "acceptable according to what a man has, not according to what he does not have" (II Cor. 8:12).

Simply stated, the final judgment will be rendered in accordance with what each of us has done as to insight, gifts, and capacity, not upon those things inaccessible through inadvertence. Any penalty God renders will be inflicted as behavior and justice demands. The divine principles of love, equity and mercy clearly suggest the need for individual assessment in judgment, according to response to available light, as well as God-given ability and opportunity.

Justice demands that a punishment fits the offense. A murderer is not fined only $20, nor is a speeder five miles over the limit sentenced to prison. The Law of Moses itself recognized varying degrees of punishment depending upon the transgression. The guilty man who deserved to be beaten would not be given more than 40 strokes (Deut. 25:2-3). The Jews were so careful not to impose a sentence beyond this limit that they would stop at 39, for fear of a miscount. Lesser was considered preferable to greater with regard to the administering of painful punishment. "For petty offences the Jews in many cases inflicted so few as four, five and six stripes" (Adam Clarke, *Clarke's Commentary*, vol. 5, p. 445). It is always true that mercy can afford to smile at judgment (see Jas. 2:13).

As Jesus states, some will be beaten with many lashes at the final judgment, whereas others with just few (Luke 12:47-48). This concept is further developed in Jesus' rebuke of the inhabitants of Capernaum and Bethsaida; he stated that it will be more bearable for Sodom on the day of judgment than for you [Jewish communities]" (Matt. 11:21-24). More bearable? Less bearable? Here, degrees or grades of punishment are distinct, differing according to opportunity. Similarly, there are measures of accountability in response to degrees of revelatory light.

Through this light God radiates His divine nature, reflecting His creation, His moral will for all. King David declared, "The heavens declare the glory of God; the skies proclaim the work of His hands. Day after day they pour forth speech; night after night they display knowledge. There is no speech or language where their voice is not heard. Their voice goes out into all the earth, their words to the ends of the world" (Psa. 19:1-4). The psalmist's words comport well with Paul's, who wrote that "what may be known about God is plain ... For since the creation of the world God's invisible qualities, His eternal power and divine nature have been clearly seen, being understood from what has been made, so that men are without excuse" (Rom. 1:19-20).

Stated H. Leo Boles, "It seems that people will be treated according to their opportunities and the light which they have. Opportunity and ability measure responsibility; some have greater opportunities or abilities than others, therefore responsibility varies. So it seems that the reward and punishment will vary according to the responsibilities" (*Commentary on Luke*, p. 262).

In Romans 2, Paul spoke of this principle which the Father will apply at the great judgment to come. If punishment is deemed necessary for offenses committed, such "punishment will be proportioned to the powers, gifts, opportunities and knowledge of the offender" wrote Boles. Adam Clarke aptly concluded, "Those who have had much light, or the opportunity of receiving much, and have not improved it to their own salvation, and to the good of others, shall receive punishment proportioned to the light they have abused."

At the future end-time each person will be measured, not by a similar biblical standard, but against his own response to a lifetime of truth received in whatever form. Billions of people have lived without specific biblical knowledge of Jesus Christ as God's supreme revelation and avenue of salvation. These people will receive a positive reward through their trusting response to what they know of God. This is because our God has written moral principles into every human conscience that everyone is held accountable and without excuse at the future judgment. All are accorded a present acceptability (salvation) by positively responding to the light received.

Ellen White wrote: "Among the heathen are those who worship God ignorantly, those to whom the light is never brought by human instrumentality, yet they will not perish. Though ignorant of the written law of God, they have heard His voice speaking to them in nature, and have done the things that the law has required (Rom. 2:14-15). Their works are evidence that God has touched their hearts, and they are recognized as His children." And so, they may never believe in Christ, but still he is their salvation.

Indeed, Jesus is the savior of the world and expiator of the sins of all (I John 2:2; I Tim. 4:10, 2:6); his one act of righteousness resulted in justification to life to "all men" (Rom. 5:18)—excepting those many individuals who knowingly reject their fund of known truth.

SYMPATHIZING WITH NOT KNOWING

As our supreme High Priest who has passed through the highest heavens, Jesus makes allowances for the weaknesses of people of faith in God, at any time and any place, and (as a man himself of the blood line of Abraham) fully understands their unawareness of sin when they go astray. While in this world he was trustworthy and completely like his brothers, so that after his resurrection he could become the merciful, faithful High Priest (Heb. 2:17-18). Sympathy does not extend to the unrepentant who in willful disregard to God's will are not sorry for their open-eyed acts of disobedience of known truth, in cool detachment from God.

The sacrifice was available in ancient Israel only in behalf of an unknowing person who sinned "through ignorance against any of the commandments of the Lord..." (Lev. 4:2,13). This is echoed in Numbers 15:22-31, where the requisite sacrifices are offered for sins "if ought be committed through ignorance." More than merely a lack of knowledge, these are done by anyone in over mastering temptation is swept away in an impulse or passion. The person still generally seeks the Shepherd, but in a moment has strayed like a lost farm animal (Psa. 119:176).

Hebrews 5:1-2 states that every Levitical high priest offered both gifts and sacrifices for sins. He dealt gently with the uninformed and misguided, since he himself also was beset with weakness. The earthly high priest conducted sacrifices for both the people and also for himself. He had to share in the sufferings of the people and feel compassion for them.

The twin qualifications for the office of High Priest were divine appointment and human sympathy. As a judge he had to discern between inadvertent, unintentional shortcomings and defiant rebellion against God. These are calculating sins committed by those who wander into faithless ways and must be brought back (Luke 15:11-32, Isa. 53:6).

In contrast, Numbers 15:30-31 states, "The soul that doeth out presumptively...shall be cut off from among his people. Because he hath despised the word of the Lord...that soul shall be utterly cut off. He shall die" (Deut. 17:12). Thus, deliberate, callous transgression of God's ways did not find its atonement in sacrifice. This is sin "with a high hand," a calculated violation. Even the author of Hebrews wrote that "if we sin willfully [willingly] after that we have received the knowledge of the truth, there remained no more sacrifice for sins" (Heb. 10:26). Willful disobedience never leads to pardon.

Since continuing in sin ultimately erects a barrier between man and God, the priest offered restoring sacrifices and offerings which removed the estrangement. Sins of ignorance and weakness could be atoned for. The wayward may be short in respect to knowledge possessed, and in response the priest "measured his feelings," showed compassion. The earthly priest had to be compassed with infirmity, sympathy. He had to be moderate and tender in judgment of another. That is what a judge does.

There was no room for self-righteousness by the priest, for behind his sacred vestments (as described in Exodus 28:1-43), the high priest himself might be clothed with weaknesses, or have a moral imperfection just like any other citizen among Israel.

As advocate and intercessor, the earthly high priest had to deal gently with the people. The ignorant are "not knowing," and do not understand, even as the disciples more than occasionally failed to grasp Jesus' teaching (Matt. 15:10, 16:6-11, 19:10; Mark 9:6, 10, 32-33; Luke 24:25; John 6:51-58). Atonement for these sins was required as a means of educating their moral perception, showing that unsuspected sin might linger.

But much more glorious and compassionate is Christ in the heavenly Melchizedek priesthood, who from God's right hand continually sympathizes with the ignorant and the weak as did the Levites of ancient Israel. Our Lord sees the evil when people do not. In this work Jesus displays the very essence of righteous judgment, understanding and forgiveness.

These outpourings of heavenly mercy fall upon the righteous of all nations. In every time and place, God comforts all who profess faith in the Lord, covenanters and Gentiles alike, who seek to live to the best of their ability in their current understanding and opportunities, in accordance with moral truths understood. These are also are "brethren" with whom Jesus in full fellowship continually comforts and sympathizes, though they do not know him directly (Matt. 25:37-40, 44-45).

Let us therefore not limit God's mercy and the extent which the atoning blood of Christ is applied. Assigning the blessing only to baptized believers is intuitively shortsighted, biblically questionable. All moral people of character everywhere who respect God are favored by him and partake of Jesus' intercessory role as they live in their present truth and light under Natural Law.

In Athens Paul found an alter with an inscription to the unknown God (Acts 17:23).

CHAPTER TWELVE

KNOWLEDGE AND
ACCOUNTABILITY

John 9:39-41, 15:22, together with Luke 12:48b, display a universal principle: the merciful God in heaven does not condemn anyone who has not had a chance first to know Him and His will in order to obey, at any time or place, whether before or after the cross. Surely there is a huge difference between lacking an opportunity to hear the gospel of Christ and refusing to accept it after hearing it.

When disputing with strict Pharisees after healing a blind man, Jesus taught that no guilt is charged to anyone who is not deliberately ignorant of truths about God. Indeed, Jesus went about teaching so that those who do not see may see, and that others who claimed to see should be regarded as blind. After the Pharisees inquired of him, "Are we blind, too [of certain truths]," Jesus answered, " If you were blind, you would not be guilty of sin; but now that you claim you can see, your guilt remains" (John 9:40-41).

And so, Jesus affirmed that no condemning guilt accrues when a person is unavoidably blind to a truth. When anyone of sincere heart and love for God never had an occasion to hear and respond to instructions from God, no sin is imputed. This was explicitly taught by Jesus in John 15:22: "If I had not come and spoken to them [the world, vv. 18-19, 21], they would not be guilty of sin. Now, however, they have no excuse for their sin [because they had heard the teaching]." Therefore, accountability to God comes only after understanding His will after hearing it.

Indeed, God will exact retribution upon every person who lightly esteems the truth, "dealing out vengeance to those who...do not obey the gospel of our

Lord Jesus" (II Thess. 1:8). Obvious exceptions are the retarded, the mentally incompetent, infants and children. However, anyone who lacks opportunities likewise cannot be expected to obey what they have never been exposed to, for God has never required the impossible of receptive hearts. Through inadvertence they have never been in a place where God's saving gospel was preached.

Throughout the last two millennia of time billions of people have died without an opportunity to obey God through hearing, believing and being baptized. The doers of right among the nations adhere to known truths by acknowledging the existence of God through the creation and possessing an excused conscience, but could not honor and glorify His son because none of these had ever been reached with the good news of Jesus. Nevertheless, the blood of Christ covers them, even as it does the mentally deficient and youths.

According to Paul, Gentiles unexposed to gospel revelation can know the Creator when they give thanks to Him and adhere to goodness and truth (see Chapter Two). In contrast, Paul said of the evil ones that "their thinking became futile and their foolish hearts were darkened" (Rom. 1:21). These Gentiles could not have transgressed Old Testament law, the special revelation given to the Jewish nation, for they were strangers to it and the formal covenant as well (Eph. 2:12). Further, where there is no law, there is no transgression (Rom. 4:25). Instead, the unregenerate among the Gentiles stand condemned by disregarding the truth of the creation and by failing to develop moral relationships with others.

ACCOUNTABILITY

In respect to Natural Law, the principle of accountability sets forth that God will hold everyone throughout time responsible for what truths they understand and how they responded to them. Every reasoning person, whether in or out of a formal covenant with God, in the last day will be judged for his actions in the flesh, for better or worse. Sins committed are specific transgressions against the natural order of things.

Gratefully, the God of equity and justice does not expect the impossible of anyone; to be held accountable at Heaven's bench at the end of time for a specific truth, a person must have had an awareness of it. Could a person have had knowledge of specific wrongdoing with reasonable diligence? At the end-time, the gracious Judge will not raise a matter of which anyone is unavoidably ignorant. No mother or father, hopelessly fallible by comparison with God, is so bold to punish an earthly child for any matter of which he is unaware.

Indeed, at the future judgment, the non-covenanter will know why he is lost, for he had rejected the moral standard of conscience and the reality of Maker of heaven and earth. His every sin had to have been committed with full realization that the act or thought was wrong. In the absence of such awareness, sin is not imputed (Rom. 5:13, 4:15; see also 3:20 and 7:7).

The conscientious Gentile can find truth through empirical evidence in his environment. In Romans 1-2, Paul shows that all people have knowledge that the Creator is and He should be sought, and everyone is obligated before God to behave properly toward their fellow man or incur judgment. Every person of an understanding age ought to know that there is a Higher Power and that certain conscious, willful actions are either beneficial or hurtful to others. This knowledge does not depend on an understanding of Scripture; God is very much evident in general revelation, through the creative order and the interworking of conscience with human experience.

As detailed in Chapter Five, a natural awareness of morality manifests itself as one "does by nature the things of law" (Rom. 2:14). This work which is written on the heart (v. 15) stems from the sure knowledge that there is a Creator-God to whom all are answerable and that everyone should make consistent choices of the good over evil. Also there must be a continual searching for truth and non-rejection of it when found (see Chapter Seven). What nature and an inner sense of ought supply to Gentiles in every time and place, this "truth of God" (Rom. 1:25) along with New Testament writings instruct Christians today. It was similar before the cross, in that Natural Law together with special prophetic revelation continually educated Israel of old.

With a firm foundation of general awareness of morality and the one true Spirit-Creator's existence, God's covenant ambassadors preached Jesus throughout the first century Roman world. Obedience to this gospel came about when people perceived that they were accountable to the truth of apostolic preaching together with moral law. In the same way, Jesus spoke of judgment on the basis of what he said. The Master's answer to the lawyer's question about eternal life (Luke 10:25-29) shows that authentic life and the judgment come through loving service to God and neighbor, His creation. For if a perfect and holy God loves our neighbor, how can we justify not loving him also?

THE TRUE LIGHT THAT ENLIGHTENS EVERYONE

In the introduction to the gospel of John, Jesus is portrayed as the life and authentic light (1:4-5). Verse 9 states that "the word was the true light that enlightens all men; and he was coming into the world." The NJB renders it, "The true light, that enlightens every man, was coming into the world." Or alternatively, "the true light which coming into the world, enlightens every man" (NRSV). The structure "coming into the world" is found throughout John's gospel (3:19, 6:14, 9:39, 11:27, 12:46, 16:28).

Jesus as the true light illuminates everyone, to some dimly but furnishes light nevertheless. The principle of available light means that through God's abundant grace, every person receives a measure of truth. This revelation from God is through the creation, the things made (Rom. 1:19-20), as well as from conscience and human experience, "the law written on their hearts" (Rom. 2:15). A third source of heavenly revelation is Scripture. In these ways, Jesus came to be the perfect, substantial light to all, individually and personally.

It is amiss to conclude that if any person has not been exposed to the oral or written gospel of Christ, he is without knowledge of the truth of God. John 1:9 clearly showes that Christ as the dependable light furnishes saving knowledge to all—past, present and future. Though everyone possesses light, the amount varies among individuals, depending on circumstances and ability to grasp truth. How anyone handles the light given him determines a present acceptance before God. Everybody is responsible for the knowledge of God accorded him, and only for what is understood, truth which has reached full mental realization (see Chapter Two).

God expects a faithful, positive reception to truth and reality, and He rejects only those who deliberately cast heavenly knowledge aside. These stand self-condemned (John 3:19-21, 8:12, 9:39-41). The evil person flees light when it is shed on him. He dismisses God by brazenly and knowingly refusing to respond in faith and trusting obedience to the revelation of God accorded him, in whatever form it comes. Continual rejection brings condemnation. Failure to recognize presently understood light available is akin to calling evil good and good evil, putting darkness for light and light for darkness (Isa. 5:20).

Light is a symbol of goodness and uprightness, bringing blessings and spiritual vitality (Psa. 97:11, 112:4; Prov. 4:18). Just men do not ignore truth, and as they walk in the light (Isa 2:5, I John 1:7) they uphold God's brightness to others as well (Isa. 42:6, 49:6, 60:3; cp. 51:4). In some measure, God has provided illumination for the pathway of life to everyone who has ever lived.

Jesus' earthly mission was to bear the truth, and it is known to some degree by every man. As the light of this world (John 11:9), he is the savior of the entire human race, especially of believers (I Tim. 4:10), dying on the cross for every person (Heb. 2:9). He is therefore not merely a potential or conditional savior, but is the savior, precisely as these texts read. Jesus as the savior of the world (John 4:42) took away the sin of the world (John 1:29).

As in Adam all die, even so in Christ all are made alive (I Cor. 15:22). Plainly, if all people die because of Adam, then all are brought to life because of Christ's work on the cross. Righteous people are objectively saved when Christ died for them. But God wants these good hearts to experience personal (subjective) salvation by hearing the gospel and submitting to it in baptism. In this way saved moral "doers of truth" (John 3:19, Rom. 1:25) come to the ultimate light and enter into a formal covenant with God.

ADHERING TO GOD'S WAYS

Through the moral order, righteous non-Christians can attain a saving positive standing before God in Natural Law. The creation itself is the teacher (Rom. 1:19-20, Psa. 19:3-4), together with the consciences of all, where in the heart God has embedded boundaries of morality and a yearning for eternity.

Man's learning and keeping of God's moral law and commandments dates back to the Old Testament patriarchs. God said that Abraham "obeyed me and kept my requirements, my commands, my decrees and my laws" (Gen. 26:5). Significantly, Abraham acquired knowledge of these ordinances through unwritten Natural Law. Trusting faith played a large role in Abraham's acquisition of God's will. In the words of Philo, an Alexandrian Jew and a contemporary of Jesus, Abraham's obedience embodied the entirety of God's moral law.

Though a staunch apologist for Moses' Torah, Philo nevertheless saw God's will through universal law even more so than with writings. Like Abraham as described by Philo, Paul in Romans 10:4 similarly regarded Christ's obedience as the end or fulfillment of the law to such an extent that our Lord personally embodied the entirety of God's unwritten instruction. By faith acquired through generally revealed truth, Abraham responded by entering an unknown country and ultimately fathering a son who would be offered up as a test of his faith (Heb. 11:8-12,17-19).

Perfection of Abraham's faith was a didactic process which involved adherence to God's instruction through the moral and creative universe. Similarly, Paul argued in Romans 10:3-5, as well as in 2:14-15 and 3:21-4:15, that the attaining of righteousness consisted of developing an awareness through faith in God's realities embodied in nature and in the conscience. Evidently, men can live blameless lives in virtue either through Scripture or moral insight gained through Natural Law. By faithfully adhering to God's will as expressed in Genesis 26:5, cited above, Abraham had God's Spirit which also moved among the other Old Testament worthies which are mentioned in Chapter Three. These people of faith were not part of covenant Israel, a nation guided by prophetic instruction preserved in the Old Testament.

Abraham's spirituality has a New Testament counterpart in "the Spirit of life in Christ Jesus" (Rom. 8:2) which is the means by which God delivers His people from sin. Verily, "this Spirit is the dynamic 'principle' of the new life, creating vitality and separating humans from sin and death" (Joseph Fitzmyer, Romans, pp. 482-483). It is something which law by itself cannot supply, because the

Spirit's activity throughout time has not been sustained by written codes.

As we fix our eyes on Jesus by doing helpful deeds and maintaining a positive disposition and attitude, personal faith is perfected (Heb. 12:2) and we adopt the spirit or mind of Christ. Through this moral standard, God at the future end time will judge both Christians and non-covenanters alike. Romans 2:6-11 across the board contrasts an innumerable number of people who "do evil" who will be subject to God's wrath with "the good," the many faithful people who will receive glory, honor and peace with God, eternal life. Knowledge of virtue and vice are universal and obviously are not the sole province of the people of Christ.

Romans 2:25-29 distinguishes between moral and spiritual inward heart-obedience and literal outward deeds and works in response to written law. Romans 7:6 also contrasts slavish adherence to a letter code with the freedom of life in the Spirit. This letter/spirit antithesis is in evidence in the "fleshly" mind which doggedly adheres to the letter of written law, over and against the person of the Spirit who obeys the intents and purposes of God through faith (II Cor. 3:6-4:3, Rom. 7:7-25). Developing the latter brings true peace in an authentic relationship with God, not only to Christians but also righteous Gentiles who are adhering to a current understanding of Natural Law.

This quality of saving justice is exemplified in Jesus' self-sacrificing act on the cross on behalf of the weak, the ungodly and sinners. Indeed, both Christians and the righteous Gentiles among the nations under Natural Law are saved by the life of Christ (Rom. 5:10), and thus spared from God's wrath. Jesus as the goal of the law (Rom. 10:1-4) embodied the kind of justice that approaches goodness, something found both in Scripture and in the natural order of things. Each respects God and His will.

Through one man's obedience the many are made righteous in Christ (Rom. 5:19). By the power of His Spirit, the people of faith who live virtuous lives will be acquitted at the future judgment. Following God's intent through the power of the Spirit and emulating Jesus' example leads to glorification and resurrection when he will return at the end of time to claim his own.

Chapter Thirteen

Twelve Objections to the Natural Law Doctrine

(1) Why Evangelize Among Righteous Gentiles, if They Are Already Saved?

It is asked, if people outside of Christianity are accepted of God on the basis of available light, that is, by positive response to Natural Law, what purpose is served by taking the gospel of Christ to them? Would not they be better off if they are simply left alone? If presently saved, and they reject the gospel, then they would be lost, it is contended.

In response, no one is ever worse off by hearing the gospel. If people are genuinely seeking to know God as they live by their available light, they will accept more light, greater truth, as it becomes known and understood. They are disposed to search for additional truth. On the other hand, others who have no interest in knowing the Creator and living up to His moral standard, would similarly refuse to embrace the gospel.

Faithful evangelists carry the good news to all nations because it is God's will. "How shall they hear without a preacher?" is just as vital a question today as it was in the first century (Rom. 10:4; see also Acts 8:29-32). It is the normative way of reaching people and turning them to God's ways. Through preaching is how God calls His moral elect of the world who would become baptized believers as they hear and understand the good news about Christ (see Matt. 24:31).

I Thessalonians 1:4 ties election to the gospel. Paul also wrote that "God from the beginning chose you for salvation....God called you by our gospel" (II Thess. 2:13-14). Without the teaching, they could not be made perfect (see Heb. 11:40). The purpose of preaching therefore is to bring these honest hearts, unacquainted with specially revealed Bible truths, into deeper fellowship with God and complete joy of life for now and eternity (I John 1:1:2).

II Thessalonians 1:7-8 promises retribution and divine judgment upon the evil who practice harmful anti-God deeds. They do not seek a relationship with God and are indifferent to the gospel. By failing to acknowledge the Creator, they have rejected Him (Rom. 1:32). Specifically headed for judgment are those who have heard the gospel preached, understand it, but refuse to obey it (see I Pet. 4:17).

As with God's covenanted ones, honest people unaware of Christ who would gain salvation do so by grace through faith, even when they cannot relate directly to Jesus. God saves infants and the mentally retarded apart from knowledge and obedience, since they lack *capability* of belief. Might not His grace extend to God-fearers unexposed to the gospel of Christ because they lack *opportunity*, yet whose day by day activities are as moral as those of covenant people (Rom. 2:25-29)? What Bible principle contradicts this conclusion?

Regardless of the manner in which God receives good-hearted non-covenanters, it has to be ultimately through the life of the one who endured the cross. Righteous Gentiles who seek the truth and not rejecting it stand faultless despite their non-exposure to the gospel. They are open and receptive, fearing the Creator and doing the morally right when interacting with others. If they could hear such gospel teaching and follow it, they would be made better (John 8:47, 18:37b). The Great Judge is not hard and demanding; He asks the impossible of no one.

(2) THERE ARE ONLY TWO GROUPS OF PEOPLE— THEY ARE EITHER SAVED OR LOST

Generally, there are perhaps up to four classes of people at any time and place. First, moral truth-embracing non-Christians exist among the nations, seeking God and living to the best of their ability in their present light. They feel for and do not reject additional truth it when it comes before them, and thus have "excused" consciences (Rom. 2:14). In an informal covenant with God, they are of the elect of God. When they hear the greater light of the gospel of Christ, they accept the message of repentance and baptism, and *continue* in their present acceptance (salvation) before God.

A second group consists of those just described. They hear the gospel and understand it, yet for some reason they purposely reject it, thus showing that they do not seek truth. Continuance in this attitude ultimately results in loss of their accepted state before God, and these people are ultimately lost. A third class of people dwell in unrighteousness and reject what limited moral light they have, and if they should hear the gospel of Jesus Christ would not accept it, and thus remain in their spiritually dead state.

Finally, there are those who persist in unrighteousness and reject what light they have, and even when they encounter moral truths in their environment, they may accept some and reject some. Yet in time these might hear the gospel and accept it in fullness of faith, repent of their past and enter the formal covenant through baptism, and are saved.

Therefore the gospel of Christ must be taken to all: to bring those of the first above group to the full light and closer walk with God, and to benefit those of the last two classes of people by turning them from their state of rejection of their available light to repentance. The mission of evangelism is to bring everyone to a closer walk with God, and also to reach out to those who ignore or exhibit indifference to Him, with a message of love.

God would not arbitrarily punish forever ethical individuals who, through no fault of their own, will never hear the gospel of Christ. Otherwise we could make accusations against Him of unfairness. To the contrary, God accepts all right-hearted people who respect Him, comforting and caring for them, continually nourishing them in their present truth. He casts into outer darkness as ineligible for immortality the unrepentant and all who reject the truth of God (Rev. 22:15, I Cor. 6:9-10), destroying them forever.

(3) THE GOSPEL OF CHRIST MUST BE OBEYED BEFORE THE HEATHEN CAN COME TO GOD

Tradition invokes Romans 10:17, "So faith comes from hearing, and hearing by the word of Christ," to demonstrate the absolute necessity for the heathen to hear the preacher of the good news of Christ in order to be saved. The Natural Law teaching is thought to be wrong because it does not include the salvific mission of these heralds who proclaim obedience to the gospel for acceptance by God. There can be no exceptions to this pattern of teaching, it is insisted.

In response, Romans 10:17 must be examined in context with the verse following where a question is posed, "But I say, surely, they [the Jews and Greeks of verse 12] have never heard, have they? Indeed they have," insists the apostle Paul, who then goes on to quote Psalm 19:4, "Their voice has gone out into all the earth, and their word to the ends of the world." This verse stands amid a classic passage of Scripture on God's general revelation of Himself through the natural world order (vv. 1-6). Even members of the animal kingdom are "instructors," testifying that God arranged it all (Job 12:7-9, cp. Psa. 33:6, 9; I Cor. 11:14). This ancient "preaching" is universal and animated, and collectively is a teacher, just as is a Bible-based sermon. Natural Law and the Bible go hand in hand in testifying of the spirit Creator and the moral order. Evidently, preaching about Christ is a form of light.

In a general sense, the good news of God as redeemer through His son is known apart from biblical texts of special revelation. This is in accord with the view of Christ's position as sustainer of the universe, for "by him are all things, and we exist for him" (I Cor. 8:6). All things were created *for* Jesus, who is supreme in all (Col. 1:15-17). Jesus is the true light that shines on every man (John 1:9).

Insofar as the billions of people over time who have lived and died without hearing the gospel even once, Paul nevertheless said they have heard. They have been informed continually of the reality of the Creator-God by nature, as stated in Psalm 19:1-2: "The heavens declare the glory of God; and the firmament shows His handiwork. Day unto day utters speech, and night unto night shows this knowledge." This knowledge existing in the vault of heaven is handed to the entire world (v. 4), a truth that comports with Romans 1:19-20, where the omnipresent Creator is clearly evident in the things made.

The marvelous complex of space, time, matter and energy continually discourses speech, teaching all people everywhere that the great Creator made it all. He also speaks through the moral awareness in the conscience of every person, instructing him to be faithful to what is right and avoid wrong behavior. In these twin ways, God has made available light for every man, and each individual most act upon it. Acceptance of available light brings salvation; rejection of it ultimately leads to condemnation, for such a one is lost.

The voice uttered by the works of creation together with the gift of conscience with which to make moral decisions, is fitly called "the speech of God." This is the universal truth heard by all individuals throughout time; it can produce faith which brings blessings and salvation, which is a present acceptability to everyone who respects God and seeks to ever learn more about Him. Here is the pole star of all who wish to please the God of heaven.

(4) The Natural Law doctrine amounts to works-based salvation

Traditionalists who deny any salvivic value to Natural Law insist that it is based on performing various good deeds, so it is an earned salvation by doing. It allegedly resembles the expectations of dutiful works demanded by modern religious cult leaders.

In response, the legal basis of a present acceptance by God rests upon justification by faith, as thoroughly developed by Paul in Romans 3:21 forward to 5:21 (see Chapter Eight). All of the good deeds done by either a Christian or a righteous Gentile following his available truth, cannot merit salvation or bring him closer to ultimate glorification. Still, the apostle declared, "All must appear before the judgment seat of Christ that each one may be recompensed for his deeds in the body, according to what he has done, whether good or bad" (II Cor. 5:10). Revelation 14:13 shows that the dead rest from their labors, "for their good deeds follow with them." Inheriting the kingdom involves service to others as explained by Jesus himself in Matthew 25:37-40 (see also Chapter Ten).

The righteous in faith are zealous of good works, serving as a *demonstration* of faith. They supply needs and show their love toward others in assisting them with time and money, or otherwise their faith is useless, being alone (Jas. 2:27). All justified people do the ethical requirements of the law. James 2:14-26 appeals to the heathen Rahab and the patriarch Abraham to show that faith is perfected in fulfilling needs and in dispensing mercy, preserving lives. Hebrews 11 shows that the faith of many admirable Jews of the covenant was shown by doing right, but none among these worthies performed good works to *gain* salvation.

Romans 2:6-9 should reassure one and all of God's fairness and respect toward righteous character. "Tribulation and anguish shall come to the soul of every man who *works evil*...but glory and honor and peace shall be awarded to every one who *does good,* because with God there is no respect of persons." All people throughout time will experience God's justice in judgment by Natural Law. Acknowledging His creation and leading a righteous life is the substance of a proper relationship with God in any era and society.

(5) THE TEACHING OF NATURAL LAW LEADS TO UNIVERSALISM

Some mistakenly suggest that the doctrine of Natural Law means that all, indiscriminately, would ultimately be saved. But the objection errs because many individuals will persistently reject God's revelation of Himself to the very end, refusing to repent and thus be forever lost. But other righteous ones adhering to their available light embedded in the heart are accepted of God in their present truth. They "seek for honor, glory and immortality" (Rom. 2:6, 9), and faithfully respond to truth which they have in whatever form it comes to them. The purpose of gospel preaching is to introduce these lost ones among the Gentiles to the greater light, Jesus, so that they might repent and be saved. The gospel must be taken to them so that they might repent and be baptized into Christ, and at last be saved.

Insofar as those currently accepted of God by following available truth, these must led to the ultimate Light through gospel preaching, so that they may respond to Jesus and enter a formal covenant with God and enjoy the blessings of union with Christ. God continually reveals Himself to all, thus leaving no one without a defense on the Day of Judgment. "Ignorance is no excuse where knowledge might have been obtained. The principle is that the demand of the Master is in proportion to the gifts dispensed, whether these be temporal or spiritual" (Paul Craftsman, *Popular Commentary of the Bible, the NT*, vol. 1, p. 338).

All people have been given insight, ability and opportunity, and response to that degree of light will determine their eternal destiny. Everyone is accountable for what he has been given, for what he currently has, not for what he does *not* have (cp. II Cor. 8:12). Just as there are degrees of revelatory light, so are there a multitude of shades of responsibility and accountability.

(6) Does not the Bible speak of a small number who will be saved?

It is oft stated that God's people were always a small minority, for God Himself called Israel as the "fewest of all peoples" (Deut. 7:7-8). God spared just eight souls in the days of Noah from the flood (I Pet. 3:20). Among the many residing at Sodom and Gomorrah, only Lot and his daughters were spared physical destruction (Jude 7). "Many are called but few are chosen," declared Jesus (Matt. 22:14), and these "few" constituted a "little flock" (Luke 12:32). So goes the traditional argument.

Even Jesus' disciples asked, "Lord, are there just a few who are being saved?" (Luke 13:23), to which Jesus replied that there would be "many" from all directions of the compass who will enter into the kingdom of God. The extent of the saved is a countless number (see Chapter Nine).

But what about the "few" Jesus said would enter by the strait gate and narrow way to life (Matt. 7:13-14)? The "many" would travel the broad way to destruction. In context, the word few is limited to adversarial Jews, the strict Pharisees who cast aside Jesus' teaching. He never approved of them for in nature and purpose they were "evil" (v. 11), unable to distinguish between right and wrong and wittingly were in defiance of moral guidance. Jesus here does not furnish a universal description of how many would be saved. In Matthew 7, members of the Jewish nation gathered around him. They had firsthand opportunity to accept the teaching of Jesus, but they did not receive him as Christ, the way of salvation (John 1:11, 12:48). Few among these would reverse their course of life in repentance and be saved.

These and other self-righteous Jewish leaders have their counterparts in modern sectarians who use Jesus' statement about the narrow and broad ways as a ready weapon to keep others in subjection. Twisting of Scripture to narrowly define the extent of the saved is akin to the manner in which some traditionalists use various Bible verses, for example, Matthew 5:22 and 23:33 to inject the horror of eternal burning hell for those who do not submit to their teaching. Here, fear supplants love and law keeping replaces grace. Should Jesus' words about the narrow way be regarded as a blanket statement to refer to *all* people for *all* time? No, for he was speaking of those who could say, "We have eaten in thy presence and thou hast taught in our streets" (Luke 13:27). In context, the ultimate destination after the judgment of the just and the unjust worldwide is not at all the subject of Matthew 7:13-14.

(7) EVER SINCE THE PENTECOST OF ACTS 2, ALL PEOPLE ARE UNDER A "LAW OF CHRIST."

A common assertion is that everybody, whether in or out of covenant with God, is under some imprecise "New Testament law" by which everyone will be judged alike, both Christians and everyone else. It is argued that ignorance of this law is no excuse even for good moral people at the great judgment, for God is never a respecter of persons. Christ's law is like civil law. Civil judges fine or otherwise punish transgressors, whether or not they actually know the law.

These human judicial concepts center upon restitution and retribution for lawbreaking. In bold contrast, divine principles have as their purpose just the opposite, the release of the violator, preventing his having to pay a fine for infractions. Imagine a courtroom judge telling a ticketed driver, an obvious lawbreaker, that his fine has been fully paid. Societal legal concepts cannot explain God's unique grace-tempered judicial system which has as a foundation forgiveness and mercy. Indeed, "God sent not His Son into the world to condemn it, but that the world through Him might be saved" (John 3:17).

All people unschooled in Bible truths, who nevertheless still seek the God of heaven in repentance and faith, gain forgiveness only because of Christ and his sacrifice. Romans 3:25 shows that God looked to Jesus as the satisfaction of the law broken by Old Testament Jews. The cross of Christ was the means by which the sins of every believer have been paid in full (I John 2:2, Heb. 9:28). The one-time sacrifice of Christ extends to all time in its effect forward and backwards from the cross, reaching every person of faith, whether in or out of a formal covenant.

The eternal God who does not necessarily view time sequentially applied the blood of Christ to the sins of non-Jewish faithful before the cross who had no specific knowledge of Him. So why cannot He do the same for the unreached God-fearer today who similarly does not explicitly know of Christ but still believes in the One in heaven who raised him from the dead (see Rom. 4:23-24)? Where is the New Testament evidence which brought about at Pentecost a change in how God blesses righteous people outside of the formal covenant with remission of sin?

In this manner Jesus is the way, the truth and the life for everybody (see John 14:6), and his "name" is the only one "by which we must be saved" (Acts 4:12). Verses 7 and 10 show that "name" equates with the power and positional authority of Jesus Christ as the cornerstone of the redeemed: covenant Jews of old, Christians, and all of the world's faithful to their present truth, their available light under Natural Law. Let us be thankful for the righteousness of Christ and "no one else" (v. 12), for it is his "name" which provides salvation, not only to those in covenant but also for the world's righteous with "excused" consciences (Rom. 2:14), people who respect the Creator through moral living. Indeed, the name Jesus means "God saves," and it is He who is the ultimate Savior.

That the non-covenanter unexposed to the gospel is saved though unaware of gospel truths, is in full accord with God eternal plan to compel His son to undergo the cross in order to pay the price for sin, but He nevertheless moved forward in His plan to proclaim him Lord and Christ. Similarly, God knew beforehand that millions of people would never hear the words of the New Testament. The God of heaven still proceeded to set forth divine instruction through the twelve apostles, not for everybody but only to Christians for further guidance (John 17:8).

(8) THE HEATHEN WHO DOES NOT OBEY THE GOSPEL CANNOT BE A SAVED BROTHER

"Who is my brother," asked Jesus (Matt. 12:48, 50), who answered his own question by saying, "Whoever does the will of my Father, he is my brother..." Wherever righteous ones may live, and the light they live by (whether moral law or special written revelation), if they are mindful to do the will of the Creator as best they can, given their circumstances, then these are indeed the brothers whom Christ referred to in Matthew 12:50. Though not in formal covenant with God, these Gentiles will enter into the glory of the resurrection. If Jesus embraced an untold number of these moral ones under Natural Law, let not Christians exclude them and thus display a negative, unloving spirit.

Our Lord recognizes as brethren and counts as sheep numerous people whom modern sectarians refuse to accept. But in the eyes of the Shepherd, they mingle among the one flock. Let us regard all who Jesus embraces as his brethren, for then we shall have far better insight into the nature of presence acceptance, salvation. Doing the will of the Father through unselfishly assisting others helps define the parameters of brotherhood.

Matthew 25:40 shows that these moral God fearers guided by general moral revelation are our brothers of Christ, in that they similarly display in their lives positive spiritual fruit: mercy, compassion, love, kindness, generosity, and other things which reside amid God's Spirit. (see Chapter Eight). They are never intentionally merciless, for that brings judgment (Jas. 2:13). Kindness is a virtue for Christians as well as for the pious among the Gentiles (II Pet. 1:7). Similarly, Christians do not have a monopoly on brotherly love (Rom. 12:10, Heb. 13:1). Arnold Toynbee said, "The brotherhood of man presupposes the fatherhood of God."

So, who is my brother? A cunning Pharisee lawyer posed this trapping question to Jesus (Luke 10:29). As a law keeper, he probably wished that Jesus would had given him a checklist of various precepts to obey and good works to perform, so as to merit salvation. Instead, Jesus simply said love and you will live, explaining how this is accomplished by introducing the parable of the Good Samaritan (Luke 10:30-37). In that story the neighborly one, though not a covenanter, displayed mercy and helpfulness, and he was approved of God. The uncharitable priest of covenant would not assist the helpless one with available resources, yet that is the essence of being brotherly.

(9) IN THE LAST DAY WE WILL BE JUDGED BY THE WORDS OF JESUS, NOT BY NATURAL LAW.

Tradition invokes Jesus' statement in John 12:48b, "The word that I have spoken will judge you in the last day" to counter Natural Law as the basis for the end-time judgment. Our Master uttered these words in his last public discourse recorded in the book of John, and they were directed toward contemporary Jews who had been opposing him. These will be condemned because they made void the word of God through human tradition (Matt. 15:9). It is specifically aimed at Jews who refused Jesus' teaching (John 12:48a).

Various scribes and teachers had persistently rejected Jesus as of no account, even deriding him, scoffing him (Luke 10:16, 16:14; 23:35; Matt. 23:41). As recorded in the gospel of John, the words of Jesus will be their judge (5:24, 45-47; 8:31, 37, 51; 14:23). So the Jewish leaders who rejected Jesus after hearing his words, those very truths which he set forth will condemn them at the judgment. Woe to the strict Pharisees and others who did not believe on Jesus and the word by which he manifested and bore testimony of himself.

Jesus' statement is not a catch-all to be applied to people across the face of humanity, for billions of people have never heard the words of Christ and thus cannot *refuse* the message. One cannot *reject* what they have not *heard*, for by the principle of accountability if it *applied* to all people, these truths should be *supplied* to them. More properly, it was the audience Jesus faced, tradition-steeped Pharisees in sin-darkened Judea, who will be convicted by the teaching of Jesus at the future judgment. Therefore, John 12:48 does not apply to the numerous individuals who are living solely by the moral standard of Natural Law.

(10) Paul Tells of a Time of Past Ignorance and a Command Now for All to Repent

In response to the Natural Law teaching, tradition insists that the "times of ignorance" of the gospel will not excuse even the righteous Gentile because "all men everywhere must repent" (Acts 17:30) as part of a gospel plan of salvation of believing, repenting and being baptized. Therefore, no hope of salvation should be extended to anyone who has not responded to this pattern of teaching to reach Christ, it is insisted.

Taking these phrases which are directed to the men of Athens and applying them throughout the entire Christian age and thus universalizing them, is contextually unwarranted. Here, Paul zeroes in upon the Athenians' idolatry and their mischaracterization of the true and living God. The repentance points to the absolute necessity for the idolaters to change their minds about false concepts of the nature of God.

Further, repentance "for all men everywhere" could not be universal, for Jesus himself said in his story of the lost sheep that "ninety and nine need no repentance" (Luke 15:7, cp. vv. 10, 32). For the Jews at the time of Jesus and Acts, the order is repentance toward God and then faith (Mark 1:15, Acts 26:20). Jesus told believing Jews to bring forth fruit in keeping with repentance (Luke 3:8). Turning to God among the Gentiles meant abandonment of vain things and embracing the Creator of "heaven and earth...and all that in them" (Acts 14:15). God's kindness leads still others to repentance (Rom. 2:4), bringing about a climate which might allow good-hearted people of faith under Natural Law to covenate informally with the living God. Therefore, the repentance of verse 30 is not part of a plan of salvation for the sinner, nor obviously is all repentance the same.

The ignorance charged against the Athenians responds to Paul's description of God that "He is not like gold or silver or stone or an image formed by the art and thought of man" (v. 29). Indeed, the true God of heaven will judge the world in righteousness (v. 31). Even a mature Christian with a truth-seeking attitude is still unknowing of some aspects of God's will, but *willful* ignorance is always sinful. The sincerity of the unschooled of Athens is to be contrasted with all who purposefully disregard the truth about God's nature. This vast difference is explained in Chapter Seven, so all ignorance is evidently not the same.

Tradition has evidently misapplied the words "ignorance" and "repentance" of verse 30, disregarding how these words are used in the context of Acts 17:22-31. Instead, Paul's entire discourse is about the nature of the true God and this teaching certainly is applicable to all beyond the immediate audience in Athens. Verse 24 is a Natural Law passage which declares that God created the world and all things on it, as in Acts 14:15. Contemplating the creation is a way to learn about the Divine

Nature (vv. 25-26), in view of impending judgment upon all mankind (v. 31).

Avoiding idolatry and moral transgression would be the first steps toward acceptance by the Creator-God and introduction to His son through the gospel. But makers of carnal objects in Paul's audience had to turn their backs on venerating these things, for such worship is inexcusable (Rom. 1:20). Thus, ignorant worship by itself does not condemn. It is in history and creation that all men—covenanters and non-covenanters alike—can "grope for God and find Him" in spirit and reality (v. 27).

(11) No Christian Should Play God and Decide Who Is Saved

According to tradition's argument, salvation rests solely upon hearing and obeying the gospel of Christ. It is oft stated that "we must go by what Scripture says," and not make judgments for God. Further, God saves only through the gospel, while evangelists are to preach the terms of salvation as set forth by Jesus: "He that believes and is baptized shall be saved" (Mark 16:16).

But what *does* Scripture say? Is that not what is at issue? If God has spoken, then we must adhere. The Bible indeed addresses the present status of positive thinking, right-living people throughout he world who lack occasions to hear the gospel. Their standard is instead Natural Law. Indeed, the Great Commission statement is our mission, but salvation is predicted on belief once the hearer has heard. Even tradition admits that the retarded, the mentally incompetent, infants and small children will escape the wrath of God because they lack *capabilities*. Why will he not save honest hearts who lack *opportunities*?

Since these people do not know specifically about Jesus, they are not accountable to his gospel, because of the general principle, "Where there is no law there is no transgression" (Rom. 4:15). In the absence of law it is possible to live without infringement of it. Sin is not reckoned when there is no law (Rom. 5:13), such as the specially revealed apostolic truth to God's people of covenant. But universal moral law is light for one and all throughout time. Because of this, God's righteousness is also displayed, and thus no charge can be bought against Him for favoritism. He ever is partial to people of good ethical character, for this is a reflection of God's moral universe.

(12) The Righteous Among the Nations Should Not Be Numbered With Christians

Tradition here fails to see that the worldwide called out body of moral people—Christians and righteous Gentiles with a heart for God and abiding in understood truth—all have in common the things that matter most: [1] Jesus, "who gave himself as a ransom for *all*" (I Tim. 2:6). [2] A redeemer, Jesus, who is the savior of the *whole world* (I Tim. 4:10), and [3] a sin offering, for he is the propitiation for the sins of *all the world* (I John 2:1; see also Chapter Eight).

Further [4] both Christians and righteous non-Christians can "serve" God (Rom. 1:25), and can "honor" and "thank" Him (v. 21). [5] Both can "do the truth" and possess and practice "the truth" (Rom. 1:25, John 3:21). [6] Both can "acknowledge" God through moral and righteous living (Rom. 1:28) and can "know the just decrees of God" (see v. 32). [7] Both have eternal life through morally "persevering in doing good" (Rom. 2:7, 10). [8] Both possess faith through things understood (Rom. 1:19), and [9] possess hope and can "draw near" to the Creator-God (Acts 17:26). There is but one hope, as stated universally by Paul in Ephesians 4:4. [10] Both have been extended grace by a merciful God (Rom 11:32, 5:15-17) and [11] have been justified, thus accounted righteous by God having life through remission of sin (Rom 5:16, 18). [12] Both are made alive in Christ (I Cor. 15:22) and share in the gift or righteousness and reign in life through the work of Jesus Christ (Rom. 5:17). [13] Both have been forgiven (Rom. 4:7-8).

Therefore, tradition has no right to call profane the numerous good-hearted Gentiles through the ages whom God has cleansed as they walk in truths known and understood (see Acts 11:8-9). Throughout the world, there are people who love God and are guided by the light they have, know and experience the truth and therefore share in the above-named blessings. Jesus is the light of the world for Christians and non-Christians as well, for it is possible to derive a benefit without specifically knowing the benefactor (Matt. 25:40, 45). God is absolutely free of favoritism (Deut. 10:17, Gal. 2:6), and He must not ever be accused of partiality (Rom 2:11, Acts 10:17). Instead, He consistently recognizes righteous character by continually drawing good-hearted moral people to Him, regardless of time and place.

SUMMARY

Romans 1:16-4:25 is at the heart of both Natural Law and the gospel of Christ. This extensive passage begins with the gospel of Christ (1:16) and quickly moves to the righteousness of God, His saving justice (1:17, cp. 3:21) in the creative order and moral obligations which flow from Natural Law (1:18-31). This invisible standard is adequately addressed in 2:6-9, 14-15, and 25-29. In 3:21, Paul states that apart from law the justice of God has been displayed, even as all men have sinned (v. 23). In verse 25, the sin offering of Christ for all of the righteous throughout time is established. The law is put in its true footing through faith (v. 31), a glorious theme which occupies Romans 4, climaxing in verse 15: "Thus the promise is of faith, that it may be by grace, so that the promise may be made secure to all of Abraham's seed."

This point is this: all righteous people through the ages, whether non-covenanters adhering to Natural Law or blessed ones who entered into a formal covenant with God—Jews of old and Christians—have been saved alike, by the absolutely sure way of grace thorough faith (Rom. 4:15, cp. Eph. 2:8-9). Any attempt to achieve a relationship with God through a system of works miserably fails. O' how we need to embrace Romans!

Because of a righteous God's providential care, no one throughout time has been bereft of the knowledge of God's creation and revelation of Himself, His will and nature, however dim that revelatory light might be. Assuredly, the greater disclosure of God was through the prophets of Israel and the Christian apostles who have revealed Jesus in their preaching and the New Testament documents they left behind.

Responsive individuals who practice truth to the best of their understanding, whether revealed in the natural order or in Scripture, ability and opportunity, are the accepted of God. All others who live for self in unrighteous living will face God's wrath and judgment, and in their ungodly behavior exempt themselves from glory. In rejecting divine precepts engraved upon their hearts, their conscience will accuse them presently as well as on God's day of judgment. On the other hand, the righteous respond to their conscience and the voice of nature in the heavens as it pours forth speech and knowledge of the Creator. They know the essential rightness and wrongness of actions because of a moral standard as embodied in the Golden Rule, and their conscience bears them witness.

Just as God does not expect the physically lame to walk or the blind to see, our gracious Father never requires more than anyone is capable of knowing. God has shed degrees of His light on every person, and all are obligated to respond to whatever measure they have been given. The God of justice and fairness holds all men accountable for only the light they have access to, and their response to it. Here is the hope and salvation, the basis of acceptance in the heavenly court.

If any man in any place and time truly loves God above all things, and is following to the best of his ability all of the truth (light) he can find, and is always seeking more and not rejecting any, does he not have a present acceptance and salvation? If such a one should depart from this life faithful to his knowledge and heart-obedience, would God turn him aside from His presence? Surely an affirmative response leads to a legalistic concept of grace and mercy, and misses the entirety of God-man relationships in spiritual intimacy.

Life's most fundamental spiritual obligation is to seek the truth and respond to it. Whatever the level of understanding, God wants us to embrace His righteousness and ever approach the light (John 3:21), then walk in it (I John 1:7). Truth must never be suppressed, for to do so is sin for one and all. Groping for what is right underlies a proper response to the gospel; it is, therefore, even more fundamental than such obedience.

Sending out the good news of Christ is not undermined or made less urgent by recognizing a favorable status for honest God-fearing non-covenanters under Natural Law. Carrying the gospel of Christ to a sin-darkened world and bringing people into a covenant relationship with God must never cease (Matt. 28:18, Rom. 10:14-16). Leaving people without opportunities to hear the gospel is sinful, for Jesus Christ is the embodiment of truth, the complete fulfillment and hope of honest hearts for all cultures in all times.

The standing of moral non-covenanters walking in their available light is enhanced and matured by knowledge of Jesus Christ. God forever delights in people possessing the spirit of faith and openness to learn what is right, seeking truth and positively responding to it, though imperfectly. They do not intentionally turn their back on knowledge or truth, and are prime candidates to embrace Christ's gospel if it should ever come before them. Though unexposed to that greater light, they still live up to a standard of salvation set by God in lesser light.

Let us therefore seek to be lights in the world (Matt. 5:14) by taking the supreme light, the person of Jesus Christ as the Son of God, to all corners of the earth where he may fully enlighten every man. Let us awaken to the eternal significance of accepting our moral brethren walking in their available light, honoring those made in the image of the Creator, for all of these good hearts belong to Him as well.

*The scriptures which were
written for our learning
are the special revelation of
God (Rom. 15:4).*

SUBJECT INDEX
◇◇◇◇◇◇◇◇◇◇◇◇◇

SCRIPTURE INDEX

Books by Homer Hailey

COMMENTARY ON DANIEL, A PROPHETIC MESSAGE. The author comments on four major biblical kingdoms in an effort to interpret the book of Daniel in relation to present day needs. As Hailey explains the Old Testament prophets and the consequential judgments on contemporary pagan nations, we can deduce some conclusions respecting social, political, and religious conditions of today. 288 pages, colored cover, paper.

GOD'S JUDGEMENTS AND PUNISHMENTS, INDIVIDUALS AND NATIONS. As a continuation of his Daniel commentary, the author points out God's ongoing involvement in the affairs of nations, ancient and modern. Reverent investigation led him to conclude that hell is a place of everlasting destruction—not a place of unending conscious torment of resurrected wicked people. 224 pages, colored cover, cloth and paper.

A COMMENTARY ON THE MINOR PROPHETS. The author treats the writings of the 12 prophets separately with general observations about each of them, the date of writing and the message. There are outlines of each book followed by lively verse by verse commentary which unfolds the meaning in clear, understandable language. 428 pages, cloth.

A COMMENTARY ON ISAIAH, WITH EMPHASIS ON THE MESSIANIC HOPE. Through prudently and discreetly phrased commentary, the author hopes that the reader will "grasp something of Isaiah's insight into the glory and majesty of Jehovah, to appreciate God's infinite love for the people He chose as His own." Isaiah foresaw the coming of the Suffering Servant, Jesus Christ, a truth reverently handled by Hailey. 542 pages, cloth.

A COMMENTARY ON JOB. Subtitled *Now Mine Eye Seeth Thee*, this study successfully analyzes the subtle distinctions in the speeches within the book of Job to make them clear to the student. Among the difficult problems of life is that of human suffering, and author Hailey shows how the power of the hero Job endured overwhelming afflictions through patience and faith in God to accomplish the greater good. 386 pages, cloth.

HAILEY'S COMMENTS, two volumes. The first one begins in Genesis and includes commentaries on Job, Amos, Hosea, Isaiah, Daniel, Ezekiel, and Jeremiah. The second begins with Jesus and the significance of his life, evangelism, elders, stewardship, and the saints amid a secular world. Vol 1, 347 pages; vol. 2, 384 pages. A matching set with color dust jackets. Cloth. Scripture and general indexes.

THE MESSIAH OF PROPHECY TO THE MESSIAH ON THE THRONE. This book details the development of the messianic hope chronologically, tracing it through Moses' writings and David's Psalms to the prophets God sent to Israel and Judah, century by century. Then, in the fullness of time, came Jesus in fulfillment of the messianic portrait that had been painted by holy men of old. 283 pages.

FROM CREATION TO THE DAY OF ETERNITY. Seeing God in nature, in providence and in His Christ, this book recalls the story of creation and other OT themes including redemption, promises to Israel. Studies of Christ's ministry, death and resurrection, as well as the "second coming," the resurrection and judgement, round out a well-written book, useful for readers of all ages. Indexed. 226 pages, paper.

THE EDOMITES: SYMBOL OF THE WORLD. Esau symbolizes worldly pride and wisdom and hatred of God. The historical conflict between him and his brother Jacob is analogous to the tension between the flesh serving sin and the spirit of holiness and submitting to God in righteousness. 117 pages, paper.

GOD'S ETERNAL PURPOSE AND THE COVENANTS. The author concisely expounds upon the book of Ephesians, discussing Christ, the Holy Spirit and the church in the eternal purpose of God. 234 pages, cloth and paper.

THE DIVORCED AND REMARRIED WHO WOULD COME TO GOD. This book sets forth the author's position on the subject. The author hopes that the book will be read in the spirit in which it was written—an examination of what God said (and did not say) in a devout search for truth. 80 pages, scripture and general indexes.

PRAYER AND PROVIDENCE. While prayer is a privilege and obligation of Christian living, providence is God working though both the natural and spiritual realms, providing all spiritual blessings. paper.

Books by Stanley W. Paher

THE BOOK OF REVELATION'S MYSTERY BABYLON, ROME, AD 95. Church leaders and writers before about AD 550 unanimously attest to the late date of Revelation. This strong external evidence is joined by the use of the term "Babylon" in first century Jewish literature – as well as its use elsewhere in the NT – and by early Christian writers, all of whom equated Babylon with Rome.

The politics, commerce, and self-indulgence of Babylon are compared with ancient Tyre, Ninevah, and old Babylon. The items of Revelation 18:12-13, which world merchants traded with "Babylon," qualifies only Rome as the harlot-trader. First century Jerusalem falls short of the economic power in view, nor was it then drunken with the blood of saints. Instead, it was Rome that relentlessly persecuted Christians. This book supplements Homer Hailey's commentary on the book of Revelation. 224 pages, charts, indexes.

THE KINGDOM OF GOD, A RELATIONSHIP NOT AN INSTITUTION, by D. Spurlock and Paher. The reign of God, is not a territory or the church, but instead it is a relationship into which one enters, through Christ, who rules over the hearts of his subjects, those in covenant with God. 72 pages.

MATTHEW 24: FIRST-CENTURY FULFILLMENT OR END-TIME EXPEC-TATION. This book studies the texts referring to the latter days and the end time, showing that they refer directly to ancient societies. Using the OT as precedent, the author reviews each idea and symbol of Matthew 24 and shows unmistakably that that it describes the destruction of Jerusalem amid a time of unrest and tribulation, and finally the siege and capture of the city. This book is based on lectures by Homer Hailey on Matthew 24. 192 pages, subject and scripture indexes.

THE ETERNAL COVENANT: GOD'S INVITATION TO FAITH AND LIFE. Various scriptures entwine the eras of the traditional two covenants, as also shown in such concepts as "remember," "seed," "people," "forever," and "eternal." The vital distinction between covenant and law must be recognized. Covenanters enjoy the certainty of salvation because of a positive relationship with God. They drink of the water given by Christ, and it springs up into eternal life. 176 pages, indexes. **THE ETERNAL COVENANT OF PEACE,** defines the nature of covenant and follows with what it militates against: legalism and party-centered religion. In Jesus the covenant of peace reached its final development by embracing the Gentiles. 286 pages, indexes. A third volume, **THE ETERNAL COVENANT, GOD'S PEACE TREATY WITH MAN,** enlarges upon the above themes with new material, especially on the significance of the word "promise." 128 pages, indexes.

COPING WITH CHURCH SHARKS AND A GUIDE FOR THEIR RECOVERY. Authentic Christian faith is diminished by people who negatively influence others through self-absorption and image-making. A 12-step program furnishes a release. 80 pages.

THE DEVELOPMENT OF THE NEW TESTAMENT CANON. The present N.T. books saw limited circulation until about AD 180 and were first collected as a 27-book unit by one bishop in AD 367, though few followed his lead. 88 pages, color chart.

THE TRINITY: TRUTH OR TRADITION? VOL. 2. That the three are not absolutely equal is shown in texts which show the son subordinate to the Father. Numerous examples show the two in a Principal-agency relationship commonly found in scripture. 64 pp.

A descriptive catalog on the subjects of kingdom, natural law,
NT canon, and other books, is available upon request.
For prices and to order books, call or write to the address below.

NEVADA PUBLICATIONS
4135 Badger Circle, Reno, Nevada 89519
(775) 747-0800 • spaher@sbcglobal.net

NATURAL LAW: UNIVERSAL IN SCOPE, MORAL IN DESIGN

The text for this book is set in Arno Pro. The display type is Lithos Pro.

Page design and composition were executed at
White Sage Studios, in Virginia City, Nevada.

Quality printing was done by
Walsworth Publishing Company, of Marceline, Missouri.

Glatfelter Natural is the paper stock.